street food

street food

exploring the world's most authentic tastes

Tom Kime

Photography by Lisa Linder

London New York Munich
Melbourne Delhi

To my wife, Kylie Burgess Kime, for all her love and support, and for being such an enthusiastic travel companion. To my mother, Helen, for being the inspiration behind my love of food; to my father, Robert, for igniting my love of travel and discovery; and to my sister, Hannah, for her ongoing curiosity and encouragement to pursue my goals.

Project Manager and Editor
Siobhán O'Connor

Senior Art Editor
Susan Downing

Photographic Art Direction and Design
Simon Daley

Senior Editor
Dawn Henderson

Photographer
Lisa Linder

Project Art Editor
Caroline de Souza

Home Economist and Food Stylist
Alice Hart

Editorial Assistant
Ariane Durkin

Prop Stylist
Victoria Allen

DTP Designer
Traci Salter

Design Assistance
Elly King and Sue Storey

Production Controller
Liz Cherry

First American Edition, 2007
Published in the United States by DK Publishing
375 Hudson Street, New York, New York 10014
07 08 09 10 11   10 9 8 7 6 5 4 3 2 1

SD225–June 2007

Copyright © 2007 Dorling Kindersley Ltd
Text copyright © 2007 Tom Kime
All rights reserved

Published in Great Britain by Dorling Kindersley Limited

A catalog record for this book is available from the Library of Congress

ISBN: 978-0-7566-2850-5

DK books are available at special discounts when purchased in bulk for sales promotions, premiums, fund-raising, or educational use. For details, contact: DK Publishing Special Markets, 375 Hudson Street, New York, New York 10014 or SpecialSales@dk.com

Color reproduction by Colourscan, Singapore
Printed and bound by Leo, China

Discover more at
www.dk.com

Contents

Afghani flat bread · Roast pumpkin paste · Carrot pickle ·
Toasted pita bread salad · Zucchini salad · Sesame salad ·
Eastern jeweled pilaf with cinnamon and almonds · Lamb
meatballs with sour cherry sauce · Spinach pastries ·
Spicy bean soup · Smoky roast eggplant dip · Yogurt
cream cheese dip · Carrot and orange salad with paprika
dressing · Lebanese lamb pizza · Coriander marinated fish
· Lamb kebabs with white bean and tomato salad ·
Spinach and walnut salad · Spiced roast almonds · Libyan
pumpkin dip · Spiced tomato relish · Sesame tarator sauce
· Pine nut tarator sauce · Zucchini stuffed with lamb and
pine nuts · Hummus with cinnamon lamb · Spicy lamb
chops · Almond and cardamom biscuits

Recipe navigator

The recipe navigator is organized by type of dish, rather than by country of origin. You can see all the recipes at a glance and choose what you want to make, in combinations ranging from snacks and finger food, to dishes that are more substantial.

Best in a bowl

Coconut and turmeric fish soup pp26–27

Potato and cumin curry pp38–39

South Vietnamese seafood curry pp64–65

Seafood laksa pp70–71

Spicy mussel soup pp86–87

Mexican pumpkin flower soup pp100–101

Chard soup with rice and turmeric pp148–149

Spicy bean soup pp166–167

Mexican pumpkin flower soup pp100–101

Fresh, crisp salads

Mango, papaya, and pineapple salad pp58–59

Hot and sour squid and green mango salad pp68–69

Hot and sour grilled beef salad with roasted rice pp72–73

Salad of roast pork with cucumber and sesame seeds pp78–79

Toasted pita bread salad pp156–157

Zucchini salad p158

Sesame salad p159

Carrot and orange salad with paprika dressing pp170–171

Spinach and walnut salad pp178–179

Toasted pita bread salad pp156–157

Finger food

Masala popadums with tomato and green chili pp24–25

Spicy seasoned potato in a cone pp28–29

Spicy fried okra pp32–33

Chaat with green chili and pomegranate pp36–37

Summer rolls with prawns, crab, ginger, and mint pp44–45

Paper-wrapped chicken pp52–53

Singapore prawn fritters with sweet chili sauce pp56–57

Crispy chicken spring rolls pp60–61

Hanoi prawn cakes pp74–75

Bean patties with avocado and tomato salad pp90–91

Semolina flour fritters pp114–115

Panelle (chickpea fritters) p115

Salt cod croquettes pp130–131

Harissa mini fish cakes with preserved lemon pp150–151

Spiced roast almonds pp180–181

salt cod croquettes
pp130–131

A meal in itself

Spiced grilled chicken with coconut cream pp76–77

Poussin stuffed with olives, onion, and rosemary pp120–121

Pan-fried red mullet with preserved lemon, olives,
   and parsley pp124–125

Marinated quail with caper sauce pp132–133

Stuffed eggplant with yogurt and pine nuts p146

Stuffed fish balls p147

Eastern jeweled pilaf with cinnamon and almonds pp160–161

Lamb meatballs with sour cherry sauce pp162–163

Coriander marinated fish pp174–175

Lamb kebabs with white bean and tomato salad pp176–177

Zucchini stuffed with lamb and pine nuts pp186–187

Poussin stuffed with olives,
onion, and rosemary
pp120–121

Hot wok and smoking grill

Breads, pizzas, and savory pastries

Dips, sauces, and other condiments

Libyan pumpkin dip pp182–183

Desserts and sweet treats

Sweet potato and pumpkin doughnuts pp98–99

The World Tour

The World Tour

To get a feel for the beating heart of any community, and to begin to understand a culture different from your own, you need to experience the food. In countries and regions famous for their cuisine, it is impossible to separate food from society. The food of the place is the identity, history, and social context cementing everyone together. It is a point of reference, and is used in poetry, literature, and music, as well as all aspects of human interaction. The cuisine links religion to the people, with feast days and holidays, and periods of fasting and remembrance. Regional variations bind the people to the land and the changing seasons, connecting them to their roots and heritage. The bounteous provision of food also reflects perceived wealth, but more importantly the generosity of the individual and the community. In a country such as Vietnam, where there is little material wealth, I have never met a more generous people—willing to share their food and pass on their culinary secrets. I experienced this generosity in people's homes from Ecuador to Lebanon, from Vietnam to Malta.

The best way to experience the real food that fuels and drives a community, however, is to sample the street food. The food from roadside stands, markets, open-air stalls, carts and wagons, and small cafés and bars captures the essence of life in that culture. This food is available 24/7, not just prepared because there is a guest. It is real, robust,

and a gauge of how people live and what values are important to the community. So how did I go about compiling a list of the best street food from at least five continents? Did I start with what I knew or what there was yet to discover? These were just two of the questions I asked myself in the initial stages of this book that was to take me to over 15 countries before my street food journey was completed.

I had already traveled extensively in Southeast Asia, so the food was familiar and the backbone of my cooking repertoire. My old loyalties to countries such as Italy also pulled at me. Yet instead I decided to start with countries in regions with which I was not familiar. Perhaps even more surprisingly, I started close to home. Actually, I started at home. My research—and hence my journey—began in London. This, it transpired, was the perfect place to gain inspiration from the ethnic groups who have carried their culinary heritage with them. More specifically, it was a great starting point for exploring the street food of India and Sri Lanka.

I have always been fascinated by Indian food with its use of spices and regional differences. I called my two friends Jaimin and Amandip Kotecha, who have a great nose for the restaurants specializing in regional Indian food that are dotted around London. We met in Kingsbury, and sat down to a spectacular feast of street food favorites from all over India. The food was amazing, and I scribbled copious notes

while eating my fill. My curiosity had been awakened. From this was born a long list of places that I heard had great street food and, most importantly, that I had not yet visited.

The next step was Southeast Asia. When I first traveled to Thailand and Vietnam in my mid-twenties, it completely knocked my socks off. I had never seen anything like it or tasted food like that before. Vietnamese food, in particular, is referred to as fragrant, aromatic, and perfumed. Vietnam has

"In countries and regions famous for their cuisine, it is impossible to separate food from society. The food of the place is the identity, history, and social context cementing everyone together. "

an amazing range of items from street food stalls, markets, and cafés, and so a number of recipes in this book come from this intoxicating country. Still in Southeast Asia, the cultural melting pot that is Singapore is famed for its hawker stalls. Chinese, Indian, and Malay food styles are all represented.

Where else would I go? I had always had an urge to visit South America because I love the rhythms of the music and dance that seem to be the backbone of all of Latin America. It is also the birthplace of many ingredients that we now see as mainstream across Western cuisine, such as potatoes, beans, corn, and chocolate. My journeys to South America and Mexico brought the recipes for the Latin America section, with a small side trip to Jamaica.

Southeast Asia was not the only region to exert its familiar pull on my taste buds and in turn the contents of the book. Reading *The Godfather* at an early age had started an obsession with Sicily that had not yet been fully realized. Sicilian cuisine yielded many of the recipes found in the Southern

Europe chapter. I thought I had a pretty good knowledge of Italian food, having traveled there often and also worked at the River Café in London for three years, where we changed the menu every lunch and dinner. Still, nothing could prepare me for the culinary treasures I was to find on this island, which were completely different from any other Italian food that I knew about. You can see the Moorish heritage in many dishes; Sicily's proximity to North Africa has had a profound influence on the unique food of this, the most-invaded island in the world.

North Africa and the Middle East have always intrigued me, too, because of the ancient spice routes and the traditional ways of living and cooking still largely intact from centuries past. Morocco conjures images of bazaars and spices, and probably has the most influential food of this region, so that was another "must do" destination. The food of the Levant region of the Eastern Mediterranean—namely Turkey, Lebanon, and Syria—has inspired centuries of food lovers and writers with its stunning flavors. It is also an area that is special to my father. After years of hearing his stories and receiving gifts of spices, I wanted to see these places and taste their wonders for myself.

Of course, the rudimentary means by which much street food is served bears little resemblance to the actual make-up of the food itself. There is nothing unsophisticated about the complexity of the spices, seasonings, and flavors, or the variety of cooking techniques needed to present the finished dish. Be it a bowl, a plastic dish, or a plate fashioned from a banana leaf, it is packed full of delicious ingredients. I was frequently asked questions along the lines of: "What's the food like in South America?" This type

of question is impossible to answer because the different styles of food and eating that one can find in just one city or within one cultural group are enormous; once you travel further around a country, the variety simply expands. All around the world there are little snacks to be eaten while on the way to somewhere else. There are pastries, fritters, skewers, and wraps; salads, mezze, and tapas. Soups are served at all times of the day. Stews, casseroles, and tagines are slow-cooked to blend complex flavors. Fresh fish, kebabs, or strips of meat are quickly cooked over glowing embers. Large cuts and whole animals are baked in wood ovens, grilled, or spit-roasted. Regional variations of breads, relishes, and dips alone abound. Most things that I sampled were well made and freshly cooked, and I could witness them being enjoyed by

"I often started at the main vegetable market, then the fish market or where the fishing boats came into port. Another good location was near the central bus station or railway station."

the locals. In all the places that I visited, the reality was that there was no such thing as bad food sold from little stalls. If it were bad, no one would buy it, and the vendor would soon be out of business. Sometimes I would see two stalls close to each other. One would have a lively buzz and be packed with people buying the delights it had to offer; the other would be practically empty. My choice was obvious.

When I arrived in unfamiliar towns and cities, I often started at the main vegetable market, then the fish market or where the fishing boats came into port. Another good location was near the central bus station or railway station. I would head in the opposite direction to the throng of tourists, instead

following the locals to see how and where they bought their meals. One of the best indicators of the local hotspots is the workers, who are very discerning. Wherever the postmen, policemen, bus drivers, market traders, or fishermen are communing to eat, chances are it will be one of the best places in the neighborhood and worth a look. I had many great conversations with taxi drivers in different countries, and always made sure to ask about their favorite food. I would ask where the food was sold and whether they could take me there, whatever the time of day or night. A common thread that seems to run throughout all the countries and places renowned for their street food is that the people seem to be completely obsessed with eating it, planning to eat it, or talking about it. I often ate at 2:00 am or started in the market at 5:30 or 6:00 am.

In Beirut, my friend Talal was completely unfazed at the idea of eating five breakfasts between 7:00 am and 10:30 am. There is always much to choose from and it is all deliciously tasty and handmade. Street food is fresh and usually healthy. If it is not healthy, it is so scrumptious that you do not really care.

The recipes that follow were chosen through much traveling and tasting. The list of countries they sprang from came out of places that interested me, in the context of social history and what I refer to as the "anthropology of food." The cuisines chosen have evolved over centuries of conquest, invasion, and migration. The countries visited share another thing: a healthy obsession with food and eating. It may seem like an eclectic list, and it is by no means a comprehensive one, but it is my personal street food journey through countries that have fascinated travelers for centuries. I hope it inspires you.

India and Sri Lanka

The cuisine of the Indian subcontinent and Sri Lanka has vast regional variety. From the Himalayas to the palm-fringed beaches in the tropical south, local food changes with the climate, terrain, religion, and many different languages. The bounty of street food reflects these contrasts. Opposite flavors are often put together to draw out their distinctive characteristics such as hot and sweet, or salty and sour. Texture is important, too. Also, a hot dish may be served with a cool dressing, or vice versa. Traditionally people order a selection of dishes reflecting a range of intensity of spices from mild to very hot.

Day 1: London, United Kingdom I was determined to explore further the depth and variety of street food that emanates from India and Sri Lanka, when it occurred to me that the perfect place to start was in my own back yard. London, with its large and vibrant Indian and Sri Lankan communities, was sure to provide ample opportunity for authentic fare. When you live in a large city such as London, you are often familiar with only a relatively small area. Boroughs and suburbs that are not your usual stomping ground may seem very foreign. Kingsbury in the northwest of London was such an area for me; however, for my good friends Jaimin and Amandip Kotecha it housed one of their favorite restaurants. The brightly lit eatery serves authentic Indian street food specialities. My hosts rattled off their favorites to the waiter, then added the dishes that they wanted me to try because they were house specials or particularly authentic to certain regions. The waiter turned the page on his notebook and suggested we move to a larger table that could cope with the gluttony that was about to commence. The restaurant filled with respected local businessmen and large families with members from every generation, and I was the only blond in sight. At this point I relaxed, as I knew I was going to get the good stuff, not the food altered for pedestrian Western tastes.

Day 7: Malta As executive chef of a restaurant called Taste at the Fortina Spa Resort on the island of Malta, I have made many visits to set up the restaurant, train my staff, and change and update the menus. During this time, I have become friends with Ratnesh, who manages the excellent Indian restaurant at the Fortina. When I said that I was researching street food for my book, he generously invited me to his house for a tasting. He and his wife produced stunning morsels that were common street food in their native Mumbai. Every component of the meal, which went on for hours, was delicious. The two recipes for *chaat* (slang for "street food") given on pp28–29 and pp36–37 were made with me hovering by the pan with notebook and pen in hand. The chutney had been made that afternoon, and I had to stop myself from eating it out of the jar. There was a constant stream of fresh flavors straight from the hot pan; a mix of vibrant colors and textures such as pomegranate seeds and fried sprouted beans were eaten in the blink of an eye. The whole experience taught me about the freshness and simplicity of much of Indian food and fitted perfectly with my theory that the best food stimulates all our senses.

Masala papad Masala popadums with tomato and green chili

Serves 6

2 tsp ground cumin

3 tomatoes

1 onion, finely chopped

2 fresh green jalapeño or serrano chilies, seeded and finely chopped

1 tsp medium-hot red chili powder

juice of 2 limes

½ bunch of fresh cilantro leaves

12 popadums or about 24 mini popadums (use freshly cooked or store-bought)

salt and freshly ground black pepper

1 Put the ground cumin in a small dry frying pan, and toast over medium heat for about 2 minutes until fragrant.

2 Halve the tomatoes, remove the seeds, and cut the flesh into a fine dice. Mix the tomato and onion in a bowl with the green chilies. Season well with salt and pepper. Add the toasted cumin powder and the chili powder, then stir in the lime juice. Scatter over the cilantro leaves and gently stir through.

3 When ready, scoop some of the mixture onto each of the popadums, and serve at once.

One characteristic of Indian street food is the plentiful combination of textures, temperatures, and contrasting flavors. This simple example has all of those elements present to delicious effect, and you can make this dish while preparing the rest of the ingredients for a larger meal. It is then simply scattered over the popadums before serving. The secret to this dish is that it must be eaten right away—otherwise the popadums will become soggy. Alternatively, use another Indian-style bread such as naan, to make the snack a bit more substantial.

Moily haldi
Coconut and turmeric fish soup

This fantastically tasty fish soup hails from Sri Lanka and the southern coastal regions of India. When I first tasted it, I found it very difficult to identify the source of its striking richness. It was only when I asked how it was made that I discovered that the soup was thickened with a paste made from cashews. The nuts are lightly roasted, then ground into a paste with chopped coriander stems. I have since learned that this technique is frequently used to enrich soups, stews, and curries for special occasions.

Serves 4–6

2 tbsp vegetable oil

3 tbsp raw cashews

2 garlic cloves, finely chopped

2in (5cm) piece of fresh ginger, peeled and finely chopped

2 fresh red Thai chilies, seeded and finely chopped, plus extra, cut into slivers, for garnish (optional)

1 bunch of fresh cilantro, leaves and stems finely chopped

2 onions, finely chopped

1 tbsp fennel seeds

1 tbsp coriander seeds

1 tsp ground turmeric

3½ cups good-quality fish stock

1¼ cups canned unsweetened coconut cream or coconut milk

2 tsp dark brown sugar

juice of 2 limes

1lb (450g) baby squid, cleaned

1lb (450g) uncooked large prawns, peeled, deveined, and halved lengthwise

1lb (450g) firm white fish, cut into bite-size chunks

salt and freshly ground black pepper

1 Heat a heavy frying pan over medium heat. Add 1 tbsp of the oil, and lightly brown the cashews. Set aside. In the same oil, cook the garlic, ginger, and chopped chilies for 2–3 minutes until fragrant. Using a pestle and mortar, pound the cashews, cilantro stems, garlic, ginger, and chilies to make a paste. Set aside. Heat the remaining oil in a clean heavy pan over low heat. Add the onion. Gently cook for 10 minutes, stirring occasionally, until the onion is soft.

2 Meanwhile, crush the fennel seed and coriander seed using a pestle and mortar. When the onion is soft, add the fennel and coriander seeds and the turmeric. Cook for 2 minutes until fragrant. Add half of the cashew paste. Pour in the fish stock and coconut cream, then add the sugar and season with salt and pepper. Simmer for 10 minutes. Add the lime juice and remaining nut paste. Taste and adjust the seasoning. It should have a balance of sweet richness and acidity.

3 While the soup base is simmering, slit open the squid and, using a small sharp knife, carefully score the outside in a crisscross pattern. Cut the squid into bite-size pieces. Put in a bowl with the prawns and fish. Season well with salt and pepper. Add to the soup, and simmer for 3 minutes or until the prawns turn pink and the squid is opaque. Stir in half of the cilantro leaves. Serve at once in small bowls garnished with the remaining cilantro leaves and red chilies (if using).

Chaat Ratnesh

Spicy seasoned potato in a cone

Serves 8

3 all-purpose medium potatoes

2 tbsp flaked coconut

a little vegetable oil

1 onion, finely chopped

8oz (225g) mixed mung bean sprouts and
  alfalfa sprouts, rinsed and drained

2 fresh green jalapeño or serrano chilies,
  seeded and finely chopped

1 red bell pepper, seeded and finely diced

2 scallions (green onions), thinly sliced

juice of 1 lemon

30 fresh cilantro leaves, coarsely chopped

3 tbsp Date and Tamarind Chutney
  (see p30)

salt and freshly ground black pepper

1 First make the cones to hold the filling; these will take the greatest amount of time, so it is better to have them all ready before you start cooking. You will need some banana leaves. Cut them into 4in x 8in (10cm x 20cm) rectangles, allowing for 3 rectangles per person. Roll each rectangle into a tight cone. Secure the edges with a toothpick to hold in place.

2 Peel the potatoes and cut into ½in (1cm) chunks. Place in a pan of cold water with a little salt and bring to a boil. Reduce the heat and simmer until the potato is tender when pierced with the tip of a sharp knife, but still firm. Drain in a sieve and let cool.

3 Place a dry heavy pan over medium-high heat. Add the coconut and toast, stirring often, until golden brown. Remove and set aside. Add a little oil to the pan, and cook the onion for 3–4 minutes until golden brown. Increase the heat to high, add the bean sprouts, and cook quickly for another 2 minutes. Next add the chilies and red bell pepper. Cook quickly for another couple of minutes until the mixture is crisp-tender. Season well with salt and black pepper. Stir in the lemon juice.

4 Combine the cooked mixture with the diced potato, scallions, and Date and Tamarind Chutney. Stir in the cilantro. Taste the mixture and adjust the seasoning. The seeds and coconut should provide a good crunch. Using a small spoon, fill the cones and hand them to your guests with small spoons to eat the filling. Eat at once so the filling does not soften the cone. You can refill the banana-leaf cones as needed.

My friend Ratnesh introduced me to this quick and tasty Indian street food snack, or "chaat." It is incredibly good and, like much Indian food when it is made well, healthy and easy. This particular chaat mixture is stuffed into small cones made from banana leaves. Banana leaves are available in Asian food stores. With a bit of notice, you could also ask your grocer to order them for you. If you can't find fresh banana leaves, make small cones using parchment paper.

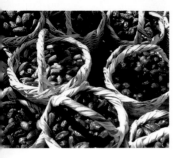

Khajar imli chatni
Date and tamarind chutney

This is a strong aromatic relish which is deliciously rich and complex. There is lots of spice, although you could add more chilies if you like. The use of tamarind and vinegar means that this pickle will be predominately hot, sour, and sweet. This chutney is great alongside roasted meats or a curry, and it is often served as an accompaniment to street food dishes, with their contrasting textures and balance of flavors. It goes especially well with Chaat Ratnesh (see pp28–29).

Makes about 4 jars

2–3in (5–7.5cm) fresh ginger, grated

6 fresh red jalapeño or serrano chilies, seeded and finely chopped

4 garlic cloves, finely chopped

2¼lb (1kg) pitted dates, coarsely chopped

1 tbsp coriander seeds

1 tbsp cumin seeds

4 green cardamom pods

2 tsp ground cinnamon

1 tsp ground nutmeg

1 tsp ground cloves

1 large onion, finely chopped

½lb (250g) tomatoes, chopped

1 cup (packed) brown sugar

1 cup tamarind pulp (see note below)

1 cup malt vinegar

sea salt and freshly ground black pepper

1 Combine the ginger, chilies, and garlic in a food processor. Process, pulsing on and off, until you have a thick paste. Add half the dates and process until they are coarsely puréed. (Leave the other half coarsely chopped.) Toast the coriander seeds, cumin seeds, cardamom pods, cinnamon, nutmeg, and cloves in a small heavy pan over medium-high heat for 2–3 minutes, or until fragrant. Remove from the pan and grind until smooth using a pestle and mortar or a spice grinder. Press through a sieve to remove any coarse pieces.

2 Put all the ingredients, including the spice and date mixtures, in a heavy saucepan. Add 2 cups water, and cook over low heat for 1–2 hours to make a thick, dark relish. Stir frequently to avoid the sugar sticking to the bottom of the pan. Taste and season well with salt and pepper. This chutney can be eaten right away or bottled in sterilized glass jars with tight-fitting lids. Store in a cool, dark place, and keep refrigerated once opened.

Using tamarind Tamarind is available in various forms. It can be bought in a block, which contains the pulp, seeds, and stringy fibers. To use this, place in a bowl and pour over 3½ cups boiling water. Let the mixture cool, then break up the sticky pieces, pressing the seeds away from the flesh with your fingers. Remove any seeds and tough fibers. Add another 2 cups water and press through a fine sieve. This is tamarind pulp. Alternatively, you can buy jars of pulp already prepared. There is also a tamarind concentrate available; this needs to be diluted with water because it is very black and very strong.

Patta moongphali chatni
Fresh cilantro and peanut chutney

Serves 6–8

3 tbsp skinless raw peanuts

1 garlic clove, peeled

½ tsp salt

1 tsp sugar

1 tsp ground cumin

1 tsp ground coriander

4 fresh green jalapeño chilies, seeded and
  finely chopped

1 large bunch of fresh cilantro, coarsely
  chopped

juice of 2 limes

1 Roast the peanuts in a dry frying pan until golden brown, taking care they do not burn. Remove from the heat, and let cool before placing in a food processor with the garlic, salt, sugar, cumin, and ground coriander. Process to a paste. Add the green chilies, cilantro, and 2 tbsp water. Process to a smooth or coarse paste, or leave with a bit of texture, according to your taste.

2 Transfer to a bowl and stir in the lime juice. Taste and adjust seasoning. It should be hot from the chilies, sweet from the roasted nuts, and salty and sour from the lime juice. Use at once.

Fresh herb chutneys such as this one are commonly used in Sri Lanka and India to accompany grilled fish, meat, or shellfish. There are many variations using peanuts, cashew nuts, or fresh or toasted coconut. The sourness is usually supplied by using lemon juice, lime juice, or fresh tamarind pulp. This chutney should be eaten immediately, as the acidity of the citrus juice will start to cook the fresh green herbs. It can be used to marinate grilled prawns or fresh tuna, or served on the side like a relish. It would be great as part of a summer barbecue or with prawn or chicken kebabs.

Bhindi chatpatti Spicy fried okra

Serves 4–6

2 tbsp Greek-style yogurt

1½ cups chickpea flour

1½ tsp chili powder

1 tsp ground cumin

2¼lb (1kg) fresh okra

1¼ cups vegetable oil, for deep frying

sea salt and freshly ground black pepper

lemon wedges, for serving

Okra, or bindhi, is cooked in many different ways in all sorts of Sri Lankan and Indian dishes. For best results it should be fried in a little oil until golden brown with a nutty taste, then added to other vegetables or covered with a sauce. This recipe is very simple and is eaten as a snack in many parts of Sri Lanka and India. When I first had okra this way, I found them so delicious that it was difficult for me to stop eating them. These work well at the start of a large meal.

1 To make the batter, spoon the yogurt into a large bowl. Sift in the chickpea flour, and whisk together to blend. Add the chili powder and ground cumin. Continue whisking while slowly adding cold water, a few tablespoons at a time, until the batter is the consistency of heavy cream. If it is too thin, simply add a little extra yogurt. Season well with salt and pepper, then set aside while you prepare the other ingredients.

2 Cut the okra in half lengthwise. Place in a colander and rinse thoroughly under cold water. Let drain for a few minutes, then give the colander a good shake to drain off any excess water. Turn the okra onto a clean towel, and pat dry to remove any moisture.

3 Heat the vegetable oil in a heavy pan over medium heat. To test that the oil is hot enough, coat a piece of okra with the batter and drop into the oil. It should sizzle immediately; if it doesn't, let the oil get hotter before adding any more okra. When the oil is ready, take a handful of okra and dip into the batter. Carefully drop the battered okra into the hot oil, scattering them across the surface of the oil so that they do not stick together. (It is important to cook the okra in batches; otherwise the temperature of the oil will drop and the okra will become soggy.) Move the okra around the pan as they are frying, separating them with a slotted spoon. Fry for about 3 minutes or until golden brown all over. Remove from the oil and drain well on paper towels. Keep warm while you continue cooking in batches until all the okra is used.

4 Sprinkle with salt and serve in a large stack with lemon wedges to squeeze over—the acidity of the lemon complements the spicy okra. Alternatively, make small parchment paper cones, securing the edges with toothpicks. Fill each one with some of the fried okra, and finish with a squeeze of lemon juice before serving at once.

Tawa mooli paratha Crispy paratha

Makes 8

For the dough

1 cup whole wheat flour

1 cup all-purpose flour

2 tsp salt

For the filling

1 daikon (Japanese radish), about 6in
  (15cm) long, grated

1 tbsp cumin seeds

1 tbsp coriander seeds

4 scallions (green onions), thinly sliced

2in (5cm) piece of fresh ginger, grated

2 fresh green jalapeño or serrano chilies,
  seeded and finely chopped

½ bunch of fresh cilantro,
  coarsely chopped

salt and freshly ground black pepper

4 tbsp (½ stick) unsalted butter, melted,
  for cooking

1 To make the dough, sift the two flours and salt into a large bowl. Make a well in the center, and slowly mix in 1 cup cold water to form a dough. Turn onto a lightly floured work surface. Knead well for 10 minutes. Return the dough to the bowl and cover with a damp cloth. Let sit for 45 minutes.

2 Meanwhile, prepare the filling. Place the daikon on a clean towel, and squeeze all the liquid out until it is very dry. Toast the cumin and coriander seeds in a small dry frying pan over medium heat for 2 minutes or until fragrant. Crush the seeds using a pestle and mortar, or a spice grinder. Mix all the filling ingredients together, and season well with salt and pepper.

3 Once the dough has rested, divide into 8 equal-sized balls. Knead each one again for a couple of minutes. Roll each dough ball into a disc about 3½in (8cm) in diameter. Place a spoonful of filling in the center of each disc. Fold the edges into the center to cover the filling completely, then give the gathered edges a slight twist to seal the bundle shut. Turn over so the sealed side is facing down. Gently roll until the paratha is about twice its original width.

4 Heat a heavy frying pan over medium-high heat. Slap a paratha into the pan and cook for 30 seconds. Turn over and cook for another 30 seconds. Brush with melted butter and turn again. Press down with a spatula, brush with more melted butter, then turn again, cooking for 30 seconds each time. Turn a couple of times more, leaving for about 10 seconds each time before turning again. Cook for 3 minutes total, until golden brown with a few dark spots. Cut into wedges and serve.

Paratha is a staple Indian flat bread with a flaky texture. It originates from the northwestern Indian province of Punjab. Here, many types of bread are eaten at all times of the day. Paratha can be eaten plain or can be stuffed with various fillings, from meat to vegetables or lentils. They are often eaten for breakfast with spicy pickles and fresh yogurt. The stuffing can be simple like this street food version or much more elaborate for feast days and banquets, such as spiced lamb and pomegranate seeds.

Chaat anardana hari mirch
Chaat with green chili and pomegranate

In Mumbai, a slang word for street food snacks is "chaat." Snacks such as this are eaten all over India at any time of the day, and there are hundreds of varieties. They often have a very noticeable contrast in tastes between hot, sweet, salty, and sour. This particular chaat is served on toasted naan or pita bread. Alternatively, you could use pieces of fried samosa dough, which can be bought at any Indian grocery store. You could even serve it on popadums broken into small triangles. It makes a striking canapé to impress your guests.

Serves 6

a little vegetable oil

2 garlic cloves, finely chopped

½ tsp crushed red chilies

1 small onion, finely chopped

8oz (225g) mixed mung bean sprouts and alfalfa sprouts, rinsed and drained

1 orange

1 apple, cored

1 pomegranate

3 scallions (green onions), finely sliced

2 fresh green jalapeño or serrano chilies, seeded and finely chopped

½ bunch of fresh cilantro, coarsely chopped

naan or pita bread, cut into triangular pieces and toasted, to serve

Fresh mango chutney

1 ripe mango, peeled and finely diced

2 fresh red chilies, seeded and finely diced

½ tsp ground cumin

1 tbsp brown sugar

2 tbsp tamarind pulp (see p30)

salt and freshly ground black pepper

1 Heat a little oil in a heavy frying pan over medium-high heat. Cook the garlic and dried chilies until aromatic. Add the onion and cook quickly until the onion is soft and just starting to color. Add the sprouts. Continue cooking quickly, stirring, for 2–3 minutes. Remove from the heat and turn into a bowl. Peel the orange and cut into segments, removing any pith. Cut the orange flesh into a small dice, then finely dice the apple. Add the orange and apple to the sprout mixture.

2 To remove the seeds from the pomegranate, take the fruit in your left hand and tap firmly all over with a wooden spoon. Cut the pomegranate in half, hold each half over the bowl containing the sprout mixture, and continue to firmly tap the outside of the fruit. The seeds will fall out, leaving the bitter white pith behind. Next add the scallions, chilies, and cilantro. Toss gently to mix.

3 Put all the chutney ingredients in a small saucepan. Add ½ cup water and bring to a boil. Reduce the heat, and simmer for 12–15 minutes or until the excess water has evaporated. Remove from the heat, and cool. Spoon about 3 tbsp of the chutney onto the sprout mixture. The mixture is then spooned onto the naan bread and eaten at once. If serving as canapés, add the topping just before serving.

Aloo jeera
Potato and cumin curry

This classic potato curry from south India is a dish frequently featured as street food. It works very well as an accompaniment to other curries and dishes, so that you have a selection of different flavors, colors, and textures. Fresh homemade curries taste so different from takeaway and those served in restaurants, and you can truly appreciate the essential, simple nature of true Indian food.

Serves 4–6

2 tbsp vegetable oil

4 garlic cloves, crushed

2in (5cm) piece of fresh ginger, grated

⅓ cup shallots, finely chopped

1lb (450g) all-purpose potatoes, peeled and cut into ½in (1cm) dice

1 tsp ground turmeric

1 tbsp black mustard seeds

1 tbsp ground coriander

1 tbsp ground cumin

2 green cardamom pods

3 fresh green jalapeño or serrano chilies, seeded and finely chopped

4 medium tomatoes, chopped

1 cup canned chickpeas (garbanzo beans), drained and rinsed in cold water

1 tsp salt

juice of 1 lemon

½ bunch of fresh cilantro

freshly ground black pepper

1 Heat the oil in a heavy saucepan over medium-high heat. Add the garlic and ginger. Cook for 2–3 minutes until the garlic and ginger are fragrant. Add the shallot and potato and cook, stirring and tossing, for about 4 minutes or until the shallot has softened. Stir in the turmeric, mustard seeds, ground coriander, cumin, and cardamom. Cook for 1 minute until the spices are fragrant, then add the chilies, tomato, and chickpeas. Add ¼ cup water and the salt, season with pepper, and cover the pot. Continue cooking over medium-high heat for about 20 minutes until the potato is tender when pierced with the tip of a sharp knife.

2 To finish, add the lemon juice and half the cilantro. Taste the curry—it should have a good balance of spicy, sweet, sour, and salty. Adjust the seasoning if necessary. Garnish with the remaining cilantro, and serve as part of a larger selection of curries, grilled fish or meat, dips, and Indian breads.

Southeast Asia

Southeast Asia gives to the world a myriad of cuisines and culinary influences, with traditions often spanning generations. Yet governing all these there still remain distinct boundaries that give each country or cultural group its trademark food. For instance, there are four main tastes found in Vietnamese cuisine: hot, sweet, salty, and sour. This basic structure is apparent in every dish and every mouthful. In Thailand, this is called "rot chart", or "correct taste." In Singapore, the food reflects the extraordinary melting pot that is this small island nation. Binding all these regions is a culture of street food coupled with an explosion of tastes, flavors, and aromas guaranteed to tempt the palate.

Day 11: Singapore

Arriving in steamy Singapore five days before Christmas, after a long and squashed flight from wintry London, was more than a little disorienting. Suddenly it was sticky and humid, and the middle of the night—but I had a limited number of days in which to ingest the food of Singapore and wanted to begin my mission immediately. One of the best ways to find the most delicious local street food is to ask the taxi drivers. I had heard about roti prata (p46–47) from a friend who had worked as a journalist in Singapore. Now, despite the late hour, I was determined to find it. I dropped my bags off at the hotel, and asked my taxi driver to take me to the best stall of roti prata in Singapore. He set off, but the streets seemed ominously quiet and ghostlike, empty of the hungry locals I hoped to join. Five dollars later we turned a corner and all was explained. A small café was acting like a beacon in the night, its canary yellow plastic tables and stark fluorescent lights welcoming all prospective diners—and there were hundreds. For the length of the block there was no footpath to be seen—only happy faces seated at flimsy chairs and tables devouring their favourite dish. And this was at 1:30 am on a Tuesday. Welcome to Singapore. I sat down and finally my roti prata arrived. I tore it into pieces, dipped it into a spicy curry sauce, and devoured. With one mouthful I knew exactly where I was. Heaven.

Day 14: Hue, Vietnam

Vietnam is an extraordinary country, with a unique cuisine. Leaving the organized chaos of Hanoi in the north, I head for the ancient imperial city of Hue, situated on the banks of the Perfume River. Hue is well kept and has a rare tranquillity. It is a strange type of silence. The city suffered 10,000 fatalities under American bombardment as a response to the North Vietnamese Tet Offensive in the spring of 1968, and has never quite recovered. Much of the ancient citadel was destroyed, yet you can still imagine its former splendor. Despite Hue's renown for elaborate and intricate displays of tradition, the most delicious meal that I ate there was the simplest: *bahn khoai*, or happy crêpes. These mouth-watering open pancakes are stuffed with pork and prawns and mushrooms. I found this dish in the establishment of a man who is a deaf mute, and expresses his love through his food. Mr. Le of Lac Tien is extraordinarily welcoming; we ate and laughed all afternoon. His mother, who opened the restaurant 35 years ago, made the pancakes, and his children all served, and laughed at my long legs while practicing their English.

Goi cuon Summer rolls with prawns, crab, ginger, and mint

Serves 4–6

3–4oz (100g) dried rice vermicelli (thin rice noodles)

½ cucumber

12 cooked fresh prawns, peeled and deveined

3 tbsp cooked crabmeat (use fresh-picked crabmeat if possible)

10 fresh mint leaves, chopped

2 scallions (green onions), cut into slivers

¾in (2cm) piece of fresh ginger, grated

juice of 1 lime

2 tbsp soy sauce

2 tbsp Asian fish sauce

12 or so rice paper wrappers (available from Asian grocers or gourmet food shops)

salt and freshly ground black pepper

Summer rolls are eaten all over Vietnam at small cafés, roadside restaurants, and stalls. Quite different from fried spring rolls, they are a refreshing burst of flavors and textures. Excellent as a snack or canapé, or at the start of a larger meal, they come in many different seasonal and regional variations. Texture is very important in Vietnamese cooking and, with the firm prawns, tender crabmeat, and crisp fresh vegetables and herbs, you have everything going on in one contained mouthful. They are so juicy you don't really need a dipping sauce.

1 Put the vermicelli in a large bowl and cover with boiling water. Let soak for about 5 minutes while you prepare the rest of the filling.

2 Thinly slice the cucumber, leaving the seeds in the center untouched. Stack the cucumber slices, then cut into thin matchsticks. If wrapping your summer rolls in a cone shape, leave the prawns whole; if using the more traditional cylinder spring-roll shape, halve or finely slice if large. Mix everything except the vermicelli and rice paper wrappers in a bowl. Drain the vermicelli, cut into smaller lengths using kitchen scissors, and add to the bowl. Season with salt and pepper, and mix again. Adjust seasoning.

3 Soak the rice paper wrappers, about 5 at a time, in warm water for 20 seconds or until softened. (Be careful they don't stick together, as they tear easily.) Lay out 4 or 5 wrappers side by side on a clean damp tea towel on a flat surface—this keeps the wrappers pliable. Place a tablespoon or so of the filling on each wrapper about 1in (2.5cm) from the bottom edge and in the center, leaving 1–2in (2.5–5cm) of wrapper on either side. To make a cone, fold one side of the wrapper toward the center; to make a more traditional spring roll, fold both sides toward the center. Fold the bottom edge facing you over the top of the mixture and, using firm pressure, roll up so the filling is enclosed. (Top the cones with a little extra filling if needed.) Place on a tray covered with another clean damp cloth. Repeat the process with the remaining wraps and filling. To prevent the wrappers drying out, cover tightly with plastic wrap until needed.

Roti prata Chicken-stuffed flat bread

Makes 12–14

3⅓ cups all-purpose flour, sifted	1 tsp ground cinnamon
1 tsp sea salt	1 tsp ground coriander
1 tsp sugar	8oz (225g) shredded cooked chicken
¼ cup lukewarm milk	2 onions, finely chopped
12 tbsp (6oz) melted butter	3 tomatoes, finely chopped
2 fresh green jalapeño or serrano chilies,	a little beaten egg for brushing
seeded and finely chopped	a little vegetable oil
2 garlic cloves, finely chopped	salt and freshly ground black pepper

1 Combine the flour, salt, and sugar in a mixing bowl. Add ½ cup lukewarm water, the milk, and 2 tbsp of the melted butter, and combine. Knead gently with your hands for about 7 minutes, adding more water or flour as needed to create a soft dough. Pinch off pieces the size of large limes and shape into balls. Roll in the remaining melted butter to coat, then place on a plate. Cover with plastic wrap, and let stand in a cool place for about 45 minutes.

2 For the stuffing, heat a little oil in a frying pan over medium-high heat. Cook the chilies, garlic, cinnamon, and coriander for 2 minutes until fragrant. Stir in the chicken, onion, tomato, and salt and pepper to taste. Set aside.

3 Lightly grease a large chopping board with some of the melted butter. Place a dough ball on the board, dab with a little more melted butter, flatten slightly with your fingers, then stretch the dough outwards, working from the center to the edge, until you have a circle of even thickness about 6in (15cm) in diameter. Repeat with the remaining dough balls, making them as thin as possible without tearing the pastry. Brush with a little beaten egg. Put a heaping tablespoon of stuffing on the bottom half of each dough circle in a half-moon shape, leaving a little lip at the bottom so they can be sealed. Fold over the top half of the dough to make half-moon parcels. Seal the parcels, making sure no air bubbles remain. Flute the edges of the dough using your thumb and forefinger.

4 Heat a heavy frying pan over medium-high heat. Drop a couple of the roti parcels into the frying pan and cook for 2–3 minutes on each side until golden. Drain on paper towels. Continue frying in batches of 2 or 3 until all of the parcels are cooked. Serve hot, accompanied by a bowl of the curry sauce on p48.

Roti prata, based on the legendary Indian flat bread, has near cult status in Singapore. People from all the island's cultures and nationalities enjoy this street food taste sensation. At the tiny café where I first enjoyed it I saw Malays, Indonesians, Chinese, and Indians, and I was not the only Westerner. It is often served with a bowl of curry sauce (see p48) or fresh cilantro or coconut chutney. The bowl of the condiment is usually much bigger than the flat bread that you have to mop up the great sauce, so the only thing to do is to order another roti prata …

Gulai ayam Creamy coconut curry sauce

Serves 6–8

2 garlic cloves, halved	1 tsp fennel seeds
2in (5cm) piece of fresh ginger	1¼in (3cm) piece of cinnamon stick
4 fresh red jalapeño or serrano chilies, seeded and finely chopped	¼ tsp ground nutmeg
	1 tsp ground turmeric
10 whole macadamia nuts or cashew nuts	a little vegetable oil
15 shallots or 3 scallions (green onions), finely chopped	1 can (14fl oz) coconut milk
	juice of ½ lemon
1 tbsp coriander seeds	salt and freshly ground black pepper
2 tsp cumin seeds	

This curry sauce is the classic accompaniment to roti prata (see p46–7). The use of coconut cream betrays its Malay and Singaporean roots. A great dipping sauce, it can also be used as the base for cooking anything from chicken or prawns to seasonal vegetables.

1 Using a pestle and mortar, pound the garlic, ginger, and chilies. Add the macadamia nuts and pound into a paste, then add the shallots and pound until smooth.

2 In a heavy frying pan over medium-high heat, dry-roast the coriander seeds, cumin seeds, fennel seeds, and cinnamon stick for 1 minute. Add the nutmeg and turmeric, and cook for 1 minute longer, until fragrant. Remove the spices from the pan, and grind to a fine powder using a pestle and mortar, or a spice grinder.

3 Using the same pan, cook the shallot paste in a little oil over medium-high heat for 3–4 minutes. Add the ground toasted spices, and continue cooking for another 3 minutes. (If you are using this sauce for chicken, vegetables, or prawns, add them now and stir to coat with the spices.) Add the coconut milk and bring to a boil. Season well with salt and pepper. Reduce the heat, and simmer for 10 minutes until the sauce is thickened. Add the lemon juice and check the seasoning. Adjust to suit your taste if necessary. There should be a sweet richness from the coconut milk and macadamia nuts, while the spices and chilies will be hot. The lemon juice cuts the rich fattiness.

4 Transfer to a small serving bowl if using as a dipping sauce for roti prata (p46–47). Serve warm or hot. (This sauce can be made in advance and reheated gently when needed.)

Sate sapi Indonesian beef saté skewers

Serves 6

2¼lb (1kg) beef rump, cut into
    1in (2.5cm) cubes

½ tsp ground turmeric

4 lime leaves, roughly chopped (if not
    available, use the grated zest of 1 lime)

2 stalks lemongrass

1 tsp sea salt

1 tbsp tamarind pulp (see p30)

1 tbsp flour

For the spice paste

1 tbsp coriander seeds

1 tsp cumin seeds

1 tsp freshly ground black pepper

5 fresh red jalapeño or serrano chilies,
    seeded and finely chopped

3 garlic cloves, halved

2in (5cm) piece of fresh ginger,
    finely chopped

4 shallots, finely chopped

1 tsp ground turmeric

a little vegetable oil

There are many varieties of saté, and they appear in Thailand and Vietnam, and throughout Singapore, Malaysia, and Indonesia. You can make saté using chicken, beef, or pork. This delicious version is included because it is quite different from how many people usually perceive saté.

1 You will need about 25 bamboo skewers. Soak them in cold water for at least an hour before threading the beef onto them, so that they do not burn.

2 Put the beef in a large glass or ceramic dish. Combine the turmeric, lime leaf, lemongrass, salt, and tamarind pulp. Use it to coat the beef, and marinate in the refrigerator for at least 4 hours or preferably overnight.

3 Dry-roast the coriander and cumin seeds in a small frying pan over medium-high heat for 2 minutes until fragrant. Using a pestle and mortar, grind into a fine powder, then add the pepper and chilies. Continue to work until smooth, adding the garlic, ginger, shallot, and turmeric in that order. Add a splash of water to make a smooth paste. Heat a little vegetable oil in a wok over medium-high heat, and stir-fry the paste for 4 minutes or until fragrant.

4 Drain the beef, reserving the marinade. Add the beef to the wok with the paste. Add 1¼ cups of water and simmer for 4–5 minutes. Remove the beef and carefully thread onto the skewers. Heat a charcoal grill or ridged cast-iron grill pan until hot. Grill the beef skewers for 2–3 minutes on each side. Mix the flour with 1 tbsp of the reserved marinade to make a paste, then add to a saucepan with the remaining marinade. Bring to a boil over medium heat, and stir continuously until thickened. Serve the beef skewers with the hot dipping sauce.

Nonya sambal
Spicy green vegetable stir-fry

Serves 4–6

1 head of choy sum (Chinese flowering cabbage) or 1lb (450g) purple sprouting broccoli

2 heads of pak choy or bok choy

1 tbsp vegetable oil

3 garlic cloves, crushed

2in (5cm) piece of fresh ginger, grated

4oz (115g) green beans, trimmed

½ cup bean sprouts, rinsed

handful of fresh mint leaves

handful of fresh cilantro leaves

salt and freshly ground black pepper

For the sauce

1 tbsp sambal oelek

2 tbsp soy sauce

1 tbsp honey

1 tbsp hoisin sauce

sambals are often fiery hot side dishes that are used much like a condiment to accompany other dishes. The sambal oelek used here is an Indonesian speciality. There are many different types and styles, and they appeal to all ethnic groups in Malaysia, Singapore, and Indonesia. In the hawker stalls in Singapore and Malaysia, you will find regional varieties using lots of different seasonal vegetables. Experiment with other green vegetables such as asparagus, green beans, and broccoli. When this dish is part of a larger selection of dishes, it helps to create a truly southeast Asian feel.

1 Cut the stems of the choy sum into 2in (5cm) lengths and separate the leaves. Cut the pak choy in half lengthwise, then cut each half into 4 wedges through the base.

2 To make the sauce, combine all the ingredients in a small saucepan, and reduce over high heat for 2 minutes. Remove from the heat.

3 Heat a wok over medium-high heat and add the oil. Stir-fry the garlic and ginger for about 30 seconds until golden brown and fragrant. Add the choy sum stems, pak choy, green beans, reduced sauce, and 1 tbsp water, and stir-fry for 2 minutes. Next add the choy sum leaves and stir-fry for a further minute or until tender. Add the sprouts, mint, and cilantro, stirring and tossing for 30 seconds until wilted.

4 Taste a little of the vegetables with the sauce, and adjust the seasoning to taste. Season with salt and pepper. It should be hot and spicy, but with a balance of salty, sour, and sweet flavors. Serve immediately.

Chee pow kai Paper-wrapped chicken

Makes 23–30 parcels

1½in (3.5cm) piece of fresh ginger, peeled

1 tbsp soy sauce

2 tbsp rice wine

1 tsp spiced salt (see below)

½ tsp sugar

5 star anise, broken into pieces

vegetable oil for deep-frying

6 chicken breast halves (1½–3lb total)

fresh cilantro leaves (optional)

fresh chili sauce (optional)

freshly ground black pepper

For the spiced salt

2 tbsp salt

1 tsp five-spice powder

These morsels make a great snack and are fun to serve because each of your guests gets a small pile of packages containing tasty marinated chicken pieces. They could be served canapé-style to accompany drinks or on a buffet table as part of a wider selection. The packages' contents are intensely perfumed with star anise and ginger. You could also make them using cubes of fish or pork, or some prawns. Or perhaps you would like them more spicy, or with a different combination of spices.

1 To make the spiced salt, mix together the salt and five-spice powder. Dry-roast in a clean frying pan over low heat for 3–4 minutes until fragrant, stirring the mixture to prevent burning. Let cool. This keeps indefinitely when stored airtight at room temperature.

2 Using a pestle and mortar, crush the ginger to a coarse pulp. Take the pulp in your hand and squeeze all the juice from the ginger into a bowl. (Alternatively, finely chop the ginger, then mash on a board using the back of a knife until you have a coarse pulp.) Discard the squeezed pulp.

3 Mix the juice with the soy sauce, rice wine, 1 tsp spiced salt, sugar, star anise, and 1 tbsp oil. Lay the chicken breasts in a flat glass or ceramic dish. Pour the marinade over the top and season with black pepper. Marinate the chicken in the refrigerator for at least 30 minutes.

4 Cut parchment paper into 30 rectangles measuring about 12 x 6in (30 x 15cm) each. Lightly oil each piece of paper. Cut each chicken breast into 5 even-sized pieces, and place a piece of chicken on each piece of paper with a little piece of star anise picked from the marinade. Tightly wrap up the chicken like a small parcel, using toothpicks to secure the edges.

5 Heat the oil in a heavy pan over medium-high heat for deep-frying. Fry the chicken parcels in batches for 3–4 minutes or until the paper browns. Drain well on paper towels and serve, allowing your guests to unwrap the parcels for themselves. Garnish with lots of fresh cilantro and chili sauce (if using).

Chao wu xiang sen Sichuan-style vegetable stir-fry with Chinese chives

Serves 4–6

1 tbsp vegetable oil

1 small Chinese cabbage or firm white cabbage, cut into equal-sized chunks about 2in (5cm) square

3 heads of baby bok choy, cut into equal-sized chunks about 2in (5cm) square

10 purple sprouting broccoli stalks, cut into 2in (5cm) lengths

10 fresh asparagus spears, cut into 2in (5cm) lengths

2 tbsp soy sauce

6 scallions (green onions), thinly sliced

½ cup fresh bean sprouts

20 Chinese chives, snipped into 3 equal lengths

handful of fresh cilantro leaves

salt and freshly ground black pepper

For the paste

grated zest of 2 limes

juice of 1 lime

2in (5cm) piece fresh ginger, grated

1 tsp five-spice powder

1 tbsp soy sauce

1 To make the paste, mix all the ingredients together in a bowl. Heat the oil in a wok over medium-high heat. Add the cabbage, bok choy, broccoli, asparagus, and 1 tbsp of the soy sauce. Stir-fry for 1 minute. Add the paste, and continue to stir-fry for another 2 minutes, or until the vegetables are just tender.

2 Next add the remaining tablespoon of soy sauce with the scallions, bean sprouts, and Chinese chives. Cook until wilted, then add the cilantro. Taste and check the seasoning, and adjust as needed. Serve immediately, alongside grilled fish or meat, and other Asian-style dishes.

Chinese five-spice powder works very well with soy sauce and cabbage, which might be served with barbecued beef, pork, or duck. The Sichuan pepper it contains has a brilliant tongue-tingling effect. Chinese chives or garlic chives are more strongly flavored than the more common chives found in supermarkets. They are usually cooked to soften the flavors, and are particularly good in stir-fries. Chinese chives are available in Chinese and Asian food stores. If you can't find them, use a combination of scallions and ordinary chives.

Cucur udang Singapore prawn fritters with sweet chili sauce

Makes 12 fritters

1⅓ cups all-purpose flour

½ tsp baking powder

¼ tsp ground turmeric

1 tsp sea salt

1 bunch of fresh chives, finely chopped

1 fresh red jalapeño or serrano chili, seeded
   and finely chopped

4 scallions (green onions), finely sliced

1½ cups fresh bean sprouts, rinsed
   and drained well

2 cups vegetable oil for frying

24 fresh prawns, peeled and deveined

fresh cilantro to garnish

For the sweet chili sauce

3 fresh red jalapeño or serrano chilies,
   seeded and finely chopped

2 garlic cloves, finely chopped

1 tbsp sugar

2 tbsp white vinegar

juice of 1 lime

Prawn fritters and sweet chili sauce make an almost inescapable pairing in Singaporean cuisine. And these definitely form the sort of morsels that taste like a treat. They work well as part of a buffet-style meal or as canapés for a party.

1 To make the fritters, sift the flour, baking powder, turmeric, and salt into a bowl. Whisk in 7oz (200ml) water to make a thick batter with the consistency of heavy cream. Add the chives, chili, scallions, and bean sprouts. Mix together well, and pour the batter into a large measuring cup or pitcher.

2 Combine all the ingredients for the sweet chili sauce. Add ¼ cup of water, stir, and set aside.

3 Heat the oil in a heavy pan over medium-high heat for deep-frying. Dip a small ladle into the hot oil and hold it there to heat for 15 seconds. Remove the ladle from the heat, letting any excess oil drip off. Half-fill the ladle with some of the batter, then press 2 prawns into the batter. Very carefully immerse the entire ladle with prawns into the hot oil (take extra care as the oil will splatter because of the moisture in the batter). Deep-fry for 2–3 minutes. Using a spatula or a small sharp knife, remove the fritter from the ladle, slip into the oil, and fry for 3 minutes longer or until golden brown. Drain on paper towels and keep warm. Repeat the process until all of the prawns have been used.

4 Serve hot and crispy with the sweet chili sauce for dipping. Fresh cilantro can be added to either or both the sauce and the fritters as a garnish.

This unique salad is great as an energy-filled healthy snack. It can also be made with vegetables such as carrots or sugarsnap peas, or with roast vegetables such as pumpkin or broccoli.

Rojak Mango, papaya, and pineapple salad

Serves 4–6

½ small cucumber

¼ fresh pineapple

1 firm unripe mango

1 firm unripe papaya

1 crisp, tart apple such as Granny Smith

2 scallions (green onions), thinly sliced

½ bunch of fresh mint, leaves torn

1 cup roasted skinless peanuts,
    coarsely crushed

For the dressing

2 tbsp shrimp paste

3 fresh red jalapeño or serrano chilies,
    seeded and finely chopped

2in (5cm) piece of fresh ginger, grated

1 tbsp mashed tamarind pulp (see p30)

juice of 1 lime

5 tbsp boiling water

2 tbsp Asian fish sauce

3 tbsp sugar

1 First wrap the shrimp paste for the dressing in a small piece of aluminum foil. Bake in a preheated 350°F (180°C) oven for 10 minutes until it becomes nuttier and drier, and aromatic rather than pungent.

2 To make the dressing, grind the chilies and ginger using a pestle and mortar. Mix with the roasted shrimp paste and mash into a pulp. Add the mashed tamarind, lime juice, water, fish sauce, and sugar.

3 To make the salad, cut each fruit differently to ensure different textures and uneven pieces. Roll-cut the cucumber by cutting a chunk on a diagonal about 1½in (3.5cm) long. Roll the cucumber 90 degrees, then cut another diagonal chunk. Continue cutting and rolling in this fashion, so that you have irregular diagonal chunks. Peel the pineapple, mango, and papaya. Dice the pineapple, cut wedges of mango and apple, and shred the papaya into ribbons using a vegetable peeler. Put in a large serving bowl, and add the scallions and mint. Toss gently to mix. Add half the peanuts and mix again.

4 Pour the dressing over the fruit and toss well. Serve in individual bowls, garnished with the remaining peanuts and mint leaves.

Cha gio Crispy chicken spring rolls

Serves 4

4 tbsp Asian fish sauce

2 tbsp freshly squeezed lime juice

2 fresh red jalapeño or serrano chilies,
  seeded and finely chopped

1 tsp sugar

2 cups vegetable oil for cooking

8oz (225g) oyster mushrooms,
  coarsely chopped

2 garlic cloves, finely chopped

2 small onions, finely chopped

8oz (225g) minced chicken breast

4 scallions (green onions), finely chopped

2 eggs, beaten

2in (5cm) piece of fresh ginger, grated

1 tsp five-spice powder

½ tsp salt

30 fresh cilantro leaves, coarsely chopped,
  plus 20 extra leaves, to serve

16 rice paper wrappers

2 tbsp freshly squeezed lime juice

1 tsp sugar

20 fresh mint leaves, to serve

freshly ground black pepper

1 Make a dipping sauce by mixing together half the fish sauce, the lime juice, half the chilies, and the sugar in a small bowl. Add 3–4 tbsp warm water and stir. Set aside. Heat a little oil in a heavy pan over high heat. Add the mushrooms and fry for 3–4 minutes until browned. Remove from the pan. Heat a little extra oil in the same pan and add the garlic. Reduce the heat and cook for another 2 minutes, then add the onions and cook for 8–10 minutes until softened. Chop the mushrooms into smaller pieces and return to the pan. Season well.

2 Mix the remaining fish sauce and chilies, chicken, scallions, eggs, ginger, five-spice powder, salt, and chopped cilantro in a bowl. Add the mushroom mixture. Take a small piece of mixture and fry in the pan. Taste and adjust the seasoning—it should be well spiced with an underlying sweetness.

3 Soak the rice paper wrappers 4 at a time in warm water for about a minute. Lay on a clean damp cloth. Place a tbsp of the filling on each one, about 1½in (3.5cm) from the edge nearest to you. Fold in the two sides on each wrapper and roll tightly away from you, like a cigar. Heat a wok or heavy pan over medium heat for a couple of minutes. Add the oil and heat. To test, carefully drop in a spring roll—it should sizzle and bubble. Reduce the heat by a third and fry the spring rolls in small batches for about 5 minutes. Drain and serve hot with the dipping sauce and whole cilantro and mint leaves in the center of the table.

Vietnamese spring rolls are very delicate compared to other Asian varieties. They should be about the length of a man's index finger and just a little wider. They are served with a dipping sauce and a bowlful of aromatic herbs such as cilantro, mint, and Thai basil (which has a licorice or aniseed flavor), as well as other lemony and peppery leaves. To eat, take the fried spring roll, wrap it in a couple of leaves, and dip it into the hot, salty, and sour dipping sauce, causing a culinary firework display in your mouth. The herbs provide a refreshing zing and crunch.

Nua prik thai nahm jim
Skewers of beef with green chili sauce

Serves 4–6

1lb (450g) tender beef such as sirloin or rib eye, trimmed of any fat

2 tbsp soy sauce

1 tbsp vegetable oil

1 tsp sugar

3 coriander (cilantro) roots, cleaned and chopped (if not available, use the lower part of the stems, finely chopped)

1 tbsp coriander seeds

pinch of salt

20 white peppercorns

3 slices fresh ginger

2 stalks lemongrass, tough outer leaves discarded, finely chopped

1 head of garlic (leave cloves unpeeled)

20–30 fresh cilantro leaves, to garnish

freshly ground black pepper

For the green chili sauce

3 fresh green jalapeño or serrano chilies, seeded and finely chopped

2 garlic cloves

2 coriander (cilantro) roots, chopped

1 tsp salt

2 tsp sugar

30 fresh cilantro leaves

juice of 3 limes

2 tbsp Asian fish sauce

I had these beef skewers in a Bangkok night market. They were so irresistible that, even though I was trying not to repeat myself, I got the taxi to stop there for another taste the next night when I was on my way to the airport. The use of white pepper here means that the recipe is an old siamese one. White pepper was used in southeast Asia for many centuries, to provide heat for the spicy food. It was only after the spanish and Portuguese went to south America in the 16th century that hot chilies were transported around the world to countries such as Thailand.

1 Soak some bamboo skewers in cold water. Cut the beef into 1in (2.5cm) cubes. Mix together the soy sauce, oil, sugar, and some black pepper. Use this to marinate the beef in the refrigerator for at least 4 hours.

2 Crush the coriander root, coriander seeds, salt, and peppercorns using a pestle and mortar, or in a food processor. Add the ginger, lemongrass, and garlic; continue to pound or process until a rough coarse-ground paste. Rub all over the meat. Heat a grill pan for at least 5 minutes until very hot. Skewer 3 or 4 pieces of meat onto each of the skewers. In batches, grill for 3 minutes or until golden brown on one side. (Don't move the meat while it is cooking.) Turn over and cook for 2 minutes longer, until crisp on the outside and medium rare inside. Remove from the pan and let rest for a few minutes. Garnish with cilantro.

3 Make the green chili sauce. Using a pestle and mortar, crush the green chilies, garlic, and coriander root with the salt and sugar until smooth. Add the cilantro leaves and keep pounding until a green paste forms. Add the lime juice and fish sauce. Check the seasoning. If it is very acidic, dilute with a little water. Serve as a dipping sauce to accompany the hot skewers.

Cari do bien
South Vietnamese seafood curry

Serves 4

1 tbsp vegetable oil

4 shallots, finely chopped

3 garlic cloves, finely chopped

2 stalks lemongrass, tough outer leaves
  discarded, thinly sliced

1in (2.5cm) fresh ginger, finely grated

½ tsp crushed dried red chilies

1 tsp mild curry powder

½ tsp ground cinnamon

½ tsp ground star anise

½ tsp ground coriander

2 fresh red jalapeño or serrano chilies,
  seeded and finely chopped

1 can (14fl oz) coconut milk

5 fresh lime leaves or finely grated
  zest of 4 limes

8oz (225g) peeled raw tiger prawns

12oz (340g) firm white fish such as
  snapper or sea bream (porgy), skinned
  and cut into 1in (2.5cm) cubes

20 fresh Thai basil leaves, coarsely chopped

30 fresh cilantro leaves, coarsely chopped

6 scallions (green onions), finely chopped

juice of 1 lime

2 tbsp Asian fish sauce

1 This is best cooked in a well-ventilated space because of the aromatic fumes
from the spices and the chilies. Heat the oil in a wok or high-sided heavy pan
over medium-high heat. Add the shallot, garlic, half the lemongrass, and half the
ginger. Cook for 3–4 minutes. Add the dried spices and half the fresh chilies. Cook
for 2–3 minutes longer until very aromatic. This mixture forms the curry base.

2 Pour in the coconut milk and 1¼ cups water. Add 3 of the lime leaves and
bring to a gentle boil. Continue boiling gently until reduced by half. When
reduced, add the prawns and fish. Reduce the heat, and gently simmer for
5 minutes (the fish is very delicate). When the fish is just opaque, add the Thai
basil, cilantro, and scallions.

3 Take the remaining lime leaves and trim away the stems with a sharp knife,
cutting away from you. Roll the two leaves together like a cigar and slice into
thin strips. Garnish the curry with the remaining lemongrass, red chilies, ginger,
and the shredded lime leaves. Drizzle with the lime juice and fish sauce. Serve
as is, or with lots of rice or rice noodles, or as part of a buffet. Served in small
portions, it also makes a sophisticated offering at a cocktail party.

Vietnam has nearly two thousand miles of coast, and huge river deltas—the Mekong, the Perfume River, and the Red River. Fish, shellfish, and anything that swims or lives near water are an essential part of Vietnamese life and make up a large percentage of the Vietnamese diet. This rustic fisherman's stew has a depth of complex flavors. You can use any combination of fish and shellfish. You could also make a vegetarian curry by substituting the fish with fresh seasonal vegetables of your choice.

Char siew Chinese barbecued pork

Char siew is deliciously simple to make. It is often eaten as a snack and is available anywhere there is a Chinese culinary influence. It can be eaten on its own or with some crisp lettuce and slices of cucumber. You can even use it as a component of another dish such as a stir-fry or a noodle dish or a soup, all of which are available from stalls in places such as Singapore, Malaysia, and Vietnam.

Serves 4–6

3 tbsp Asian fish sauce

½ tbsp soy sauce

1 tbsp sugar

1 tbsp rice wine

1 tsp five-spice powder

1¼lb (575g) fresh pork shoulder, cut into
    long strips about 1½in (3.5cm) thick

1 Combine all the ingredients except the pork to make a marinade. Stir well to mix. Place the pork in a glass or ceramic dish, pour in the marinade, and refrigerate, covered, for at least 2 hours. Turn a few times to ensure that the meat is coated by the marinade.

2 Heat an outdoor grill to medium, and place the pork on the grill over indirect heat. (You can also cook this in a grill pan or under a broiler.) Cook the pork for 15 minutes, brushing with the marinade and turning to avoid burning. Serve hot or cold, in salads, soups, or stir-fries, or with some chili jam or sambal-style sauce.

Goi du du Hot and sour squid and green mango salad

Serves 4–6

½lb (225g) baby squid, cleaned and
  cut in half lengthwise

2 unripe green mangoes

1 green unripe papaya

1in (2.5cm) piece of fresh ginger

5 lime leaves (if not available, use finely
  grated zest of 3 limes), thinly sliced

4 scallions (green onions), thinly sliced

2 fresh green jalapeño or serrano chilies,
  seeded and finely sliced

2 stalks lemongrass, tough outer leaves
  discarded, thinly sliced

20 fresh mint leaves, coarsely chopped

handful of fresh cilantro leaves,
  coarsely chopped

⅓ cup blanched peanuts, cashews, or
  sesame seeds (or a combination of all
  three), dry-roasted until golden

salt and freshly ground black pepper

For the dressing

1 tbsp tamarind paste (see p30)

2 tbsp Asian fish sauce

1 tbsp soy sauce

juice of 2 limes

juice of 1 orange

1 tsp palm sugar or granulated sugar

1 If the squid is thick, turn over so the outer side is facing upward. With a knife, score diagonal lines from corner to corner two-thirds of the way into the flesh. Repeat in the opposite direction to make a diamond pattern. Heat an outdoor grill or grill pan until very hot. Season the squid with salt and pepper, and place skin-side down on the grill. Leave for 90 seconds, then turn over. Cook for 90 seconds on the other side. When it begins to curl, it is ready. Place the squid on a board and cut into bite-size pieces.

2 Peel the green mango and papaya. Still using a vegetable peeler, shave slices of the flesh, stack in piles of 5 shavings, and slice thinly, resulting in matchstick-size pieces. Put the mango, papaya, and squid in a large bowl. Slice the ginger into thin shavings, then cut into matchsticks. Add the ginger, lime leaf, scallions, chilies, and lemongrass to the bowl with the squid. Sprinkle in two-thirds of the mint, cilantro, and roasted nuts. Toss through.

3 Combine all of the ingredients for the dressing. Pour over the salad, tossing gently to mix. Check the seasoning—it should be sour and hot, slightly salty, and sweet. Serve sprinkled with the remaining mint, cilantro, and roasted nuts.

Green unripe mango and papaya are used to spectacular effect all over Southeast Asia. They are used like a vegetable, providing a crisp sour quality. If they are not available, use a combination of shredded cucumber, crisp lettuce, and some crisp, tart apple cut into thin slices. Variations of this salad are available from all manner of stalls and cafés in Vietnam, Thailand, Cambodia, Laos, Northern Malaysia, and Singapore. You can also make it with prawns, scallops, or grilled white fish, or perhaps pork, beef, or chicken instead.

Penang is a small island off the coast of Malaysia near the border with southern Thailand. Despite its small size, it has had a large culinary influence within Asia. The region is famed for its fiery hot curries and spectacular seafood dishes. There are many regional variations of the famous laksa soup; this one was one of my favorites.

Penang laksa Seafood laksa

Serves 4–6

2in (5cm) fresh root ginger, grated

2 tbsp tamarind pulp (see p30)

1 tsp sea salt

1lb (450g) whole red snapper, skinned

4 dried chilies, crushed

2 stalks lemongrass, tough outer
   leaves discarded

2 fresh red jalapeño or serrano chilies,
   seeded and finely chopped

8 shallots, peeled

2 tbsp shrimp paste, roasted (see p58)

6oz (165g) dried rice noodles, about
   ¼in (5mm) wide

8oz (225g) fresh crabmeat

8oz (225g) peeled and deveined
   fresh prawns

juice of 2 limes

15 Thai basil leaves

½ cucumber, cut into matchstick-size pieces

8oz (225g) fresh pineapple, cut into
   matchstick-size pieces

handful of fresh mint leaves

1 Put the ginger, 1 tbsp of the tamarind pulp, and salt into a pan. Cover with 3½ cups water and bring to a boil. Reduce the heat and add the red snapper. Cover and simmer for 6–8 minutes. Remove from the heat. Remove the fish and let cool. (Do not discard the cooking liquid.) When cool, discard any bones and set the fish aside. Strain the cooking liquid—this forms the stock.

2 Meanwhile, soak the dried chilies in a little boiling water for 10 minutes or until soft, then remove and discard the seeds. Soak the seeded chilies in a fresh batch of hot water for another 10 minutes. Drain and finely chop. Thinly slice the lemongrass. Process the lemongrass and dried and fresh chilies to a paste. Add 6 of the shallots, the roast shrimp paste, and a little fish stock. Process until very smooth. Scrape into a saucepan and cover with the remaining fish stock. Bring to a boil and cook uncovered for 20 minutes, then reduce to a simmer.

3 Soak the rice noodles in warm water for 5 minutes. Bring another pan of water to a boil, drain the noodles, and cook in a boiling water for 3 minutes. Drain, then run the noodles under cold water to remove excess starch.

4 Return the fish to the simmering stock, add the crabmeat and prawns, and simmer for 3 minutes. Add the remaining tablespoon of tamarind pulp, lime juice, and basil. Check the seasoning. Divide the noodles among warmed bowls, and top each with equal portions of fish, shellfish, and broth. Garnish each bowl with cucumber, pineapple, mint, and the remaining shallots cut into slivers.

Nua nam tok Hot and sour grilled beef salad with roasted rice

In Thailand and Vietnam, there are many variations of hot and sour salads. The dressing is what sets this salad apart, with its pungent mixture of hot red chili, shredded ginger, and lime juice. In an authentic southeast Asian meal there are numerous courses, arriving at the table in a continuous stream. From the middle of the meal onward, there may be any number of dishes being eaten together. A salad such as this comes in the first half of the meal. For a vegetarian alternative, try grilled mushrooms and asparagus in place of beef.

Serves 4

1lb (450g) top sirloin or other tender beef, trimmed of fat

1 tsp ground cinnamon

1 tsp ground cumin

1 tsp five-spice powder

2 fresh red jalapeño or serrano chilies, seeded and finely chopped

2in (5cm) piece of fresh ginger, sliced into thin matchsticks

4 scallions (green onions), cut into fine slivers

2 shallots, thinly sliced

½ bunch of fresh cilantro leaves

20 fresh mint leaves

juice of 3 limes

1 tbsp Asian fish sauce

2 tbsp soy sauce

4 tbsp ground roasted rice (see below)

salt and freshly ground black pepper

1 Season the meat with the cinnamon, cumin, five-spice powder, salt, and black pepper. On a preheated outdoor grill or stovetop grill pan, cook the beef over a medium-high heat for 6–8 minutes or until medium-rare. Let the meat rest in a warm place for 5 minutes.

2 To make the salad, thinly slice the beef and mix in a bowl with the chilies, ginger, scallions, and shallots. Top with the cilantro and half of the mint. Add the lime juice, fish sauce, and soy sauce. Add half of the ground roasted rice. Toss gently to mix. The flavors should be hot, sour, and salty. Add more chilies, lime juice, and fish sauce, if necessary.

3 Slice the remaining mint into thin strips. Serve the salad garnished with the remaining roasted rice and the mint.

Roasted rice Roasted rice is not difficult to make and has a great nutty flavor. It is similar to toasted sesame seeds, so you could use those instead, if you like. But roasting rice is worth the effort. Simply scatter a couple of handfuls of raw jasmine or sticky rice on baking sheet. Bake in a preheated 350°F (180°C) oven for 6–8 minutes or until evenly golden and fragrant. Check frequently while cooking to avoid burning. Remove from the oven and let cool on the baking sheet. When cool, grind using a pestle and mortar. It is very hard, so it needs to be pounded until it is broken up into fine pieces but not ground to a powder.

Banh tom Hanoi prawn cakes

Makes 20 cakes

1 cup all-purpose flour, sifted

⅔ cup rice flour

½ tsp salt

½ tsp baking powder

1 tsp sugar

1 small sweet potato

3 scallions (green onions), thinly sliced

8oz (225g) fresh prawns, peeled, deveined, and cut into ½in (1cm) pieces

vegetable oil for frying

freshly ground black pepper

1 lime, cut into quarters

½ cucumber, thinly sliced

handful of bean sprouts

¼ head of crisp lettuce, such as iceberg

5 sprigs of fresh mint

5 sprigs of fresh cilantro

5 sprigs of Thai basil

some arugula (rocket) or watercress

Nuac cham dipping sauce

3 small fresh bird's-eye Thai chilies, seeded and thinly sliced

1 garlic clove, finely chopped

1 tbsp sugar

juice of 2 limes

4 tbsp Asian fish sauce

1 To make the prawn cakes, mix the two types of flour with the salt, baking powder, sugar, and black pepper in a bowl. Stir in 1 cup of water until you have a smooth batter. Let sit for 10 minutes. Peel and cut the sweet potato into matchstick-size pieces. Add to the batter with the scallions and prawns.

2 Make the dipping sauce using a pestle and mortar. Crush two-thirds of the chilies with the garlic and sugar until smooth. Add ½ cup warm water. Transfer to a bowl and add the lime juice and fish sauce. Stir to dissolve the sugar. Sprinkle in the remaining chilies and set aside.

3 Heat about 1in (2.5cm) of vegetable oil in a heavy pan. When the oil is shimmering, test to see whether it is hot enough by dropping in a little of the batter. It should bubble and sizzle immediately. Place 2 heaping tablespoons of the prawn batter onto a metal spatula. Pat into an irregular shape about ½in (1cm) thick. Using a metal spoon, ease the prawn cake off the spatula into the oil. Cook in batches of 3 or 4 at a time, turning once, until golden all over. Drain on paper towels and keep warm. To eat, place the lime, cucumber, sprouts, lettuce, herbs, and arugula in individual bowls or on a platter in the center of the table. Wrap a prawn cake in some fresh greens and lettuce, then dip into the sauce.

In the center of Hanoi there is a series of lakes, with ancient pagodas and monuments that are captivating at any time of the day. At 5:30 in the morning, the lakeshore is packed with Hanoi residents doing tai chi and other morning exercises. On the weekend, the lakes are a popular destination for families who come to admire the pagodas at sunset and eat banh tom. I counted about ten outside cafés that were selling exactly the same prawn cakes to the many passers-by, in the same way that a fairground has lots of stalls all selling caramel apples.

Ayam golek Spiced grilled chicken with coconut cream

Malaysian food has an intense depth of flavor that comes from the use of fresh aromatic spices such as lemongrass, ginger, and galangal. It is delicious and, once tried, soon becomes a favorite. The spice mixture and method of cooking here are very versatile. You could make it with a large whole chicken to be enjoyed by a number of people, instead of allowing one small baby chicken or poussin per person. Or it could be made with skewers of chicken marinated for a bit longer and quickly grilled to ensure a succulent snack.

Serves 4

4 dried chilies, soaked in hot
   water to soften
5 shallots, coarsely chopped
2 garlic cloves
1in (2.5cm) piece of fresh ginger
1in (2.5cm) piece of fresh galangal (if
   galangal is not available, double the
   quantity of ginger)

1 tsp salt
4 stalks lemongrass, tough outer leaves
   discarded
4 baby chickens (poussins)
1 (10fl oz) can unsweetened coconut cream
   or 1¼ cups canned coconut milk
2 tsp sugar
juice of 2 limes

1 This chicken dish can be started on the barbecue or in a grill pan, then finished in the oven. Preheat the oven to 400°F (200°C).

2 Drain the dried chilies when soft, and blend or process with the shallots, garlic, ginger, galangal, and salt. Add a little water to form a paste. Process in the firmest ingredients first, then the softer ones, to ensure the paste is very smooth.

3 Bruise the lemongrass using the back of a heavy knife. Stuff each chicken with the lemongrass, then rub the spice paste both inside and out. Put the remaining spice mixture in a pan with the coconut cream and sugar. Simmer until reduced by half.

4 Place the baby chickens on the hot barbecue or grill, and cook for 3–4 minutes on all sides. Transfer to a baking sheet and roast in the oven for 15 minutes or so, basting the chicken with the coconut mixture every 5 minutes until the chicken is tender and opaque throughout, and the coconut spice mixture has all been used up. (If you are cooking a large chicken, it will need to roast in the oven for about 45 minutes after you have grilled it on all sides.)

5 Before serving, pour all the juices from the baking sheet over the chicken and squeeze the lime juice over the top. This marinade and method of cooking is also suitable for drumsticks or chicken pieces. Serve accompanied by rice, green salad, vegetables, or a Singapore rojak salad (see pp58–59).

Goi bun Salad of roast pork with cucumber and sesame seeds

This Vietnamese salad works particularly well if some of the ingredients are still warm, such as the pork and the dressing, or the sesame seeds. There is a brilliant contrast between different textures, as well as flavors. The dressing provides heat from the chili; the fish and soy sauces provide the salt; and the vinegar, lime juice, and lemongrass provide the sour. All these flavors work very well with the crisp textures of the cucumber and celery.

Serves 4

1lb (450g) pork tenderloin

3 tbsp sesame seeds

2 small cucumbers, halved
    lengthwise and seeded

1 head of celery, white center "heart" only

3 scallions (green onions), finely sliced

1 fresh red jalapeño or serrano chili, seeded
    and finely chopped

finely grated zest of 1 lime

2 stalks lemongrass, tough outer leaves
    discarded, thinly sliced

30 fresh cilantro leaves, torn

20 fresh mint leaves, torn

salt and freshly ground black pepper

For the dressing

2 tsp sugar

juice of 2 limes

2 tbsp rice vinegar

4 coriander (cilantro) roots, coarsely chopped

1 fresh red jalapeño or serrano chili, seeded
    and coarsely chopped

2 tbsp toasted sesame oil

1 tbsp Asian fish sauce

1 tbsp soy sauce

1 Preheat the oven to 400°F (200°C). Season the pork on all sides with salt and pepper. Heat a charcoal grill or grill pan over medium-high heat. Grill the pork on all sides, then transfer to a baking sheet. Roast in the oven for 10–12 minutes or until cooked through. Let rest for 10 minutes, keeping warm. While the pork is roasting, dry-roast the sesame seeds in the oven, stirring occasionally, until light golden brown. Watch carefully to make sure they don't burn. Set aside.

2 To make the dressing, put the sugar, lime juice, and vinegar in a small saucepan. Add 1 tbsp of water and bring to a boil. Stir in the coriander root and chili. Pour the liquid into a food processor and pulse the machine on and off until completely smooth. Stir in the sesame oil, fish sauce, and soy sauce.

3 Cut the cucumber into 2in (5cm) chunks, then into matchstick-size pieces. Cut the celery in the same manner. Put the cucumber and celery in a large bowl. Add the scallions, chili, lime zest, lemongrass, and most of the sesame seeds. Sprinkle in the cilantro and mint, reserving some for the garnish. Cut the pork into thin slices against the grain of the meat. Add to the salad. When ready to serve, pour the dressing over the salad and toss gently to mix. Garnish with the remaining cilantro and mint, and sprinkle the sesame seeds over the top.

Kueh pisang
Banana and cinnamon pancakes

Makes 12 pancakes

2 cups all-purpose flour	6 large ripe bananas
1 tsp baking powder	2 tbsp sugar
2 tsp ground cinnamon plus	pinch of salt
extra, for garnish	powdered (confectioners') sugar
2 eggs, beaten	vegetable oil for cooking
½ cup milk	freshly squeezed lemon juice

1 Sift the flour, baking powder, and the 2 tsp cinnamon into a large bowl. Make a well in the center. Add the eggs and half the milk. Beat well until you have a smooth batter, then add the remaining milk and stir in thoroughly.

2 Peel the bananas and, using a fork, mash with the sugar and salt. Mix the mashed banana into the batter.

3 Sprinkle some parchment paper with a dusting of powdered sugar to have ready when the pancakes are cooked. Heat a little oil in a frying pan over medium-high heat. Drain off any excess oil, then drop in a dollop of the batter to make a pancake 5–7in (12–18cm) in diameter. (Alternatively, you can make smaller pancakes.) Cook on both sides until golden, tossing once with a spatula about halfway through. Continue until all the batter has been used, turning the pancakes onto the powdered sugar as you go.

4 Sprinkle each pancake with a little extra powdered sugar and a pinch of ground cinnamon. Add a squeeze of lemon, fold each pancake into quarters, and serve hot.

No collection of hawker stalls or night markets in Singapore or anywhere in Malaysia or Thailand would be complete without a stall selling some form of banana pancake, whether made with flour and milk, or with glutinous rice. Banana pancakes are the perfect end to a delicious meal of sate, fish cakes, and stir-fries that are all packed with flavors and fiery chilies. When strong flavors and chilies have bombarded your tongue, your taste buds recognize only sugar. This is why many Southeast Asian desserts seem so very sweet when taken out of context.

Latin America and the Caribbean

The food styles and ingredients of Latin America are as vast and varied as the region itself. Ingredients such as members of the squash family, including pumpkin, have been grown for thousands of years. Chili and corn cultivation date back just as far. In the Andes, early farmers grew peanuts, potatoes, and sweet potatoes 6,000 years ago. Before the Portuguese and Spanish traveled to the Americas in the 16th century, this bounteous larder remained untouched by the rest of the world. Yet, without it, we would not have foods such as corn, beans, potatoes, tomatoes, chilies, avocados, and chocolate, to name but a few.

Day 23: Mexico City, Mexico Unfortunately, I had only a day to spend in Mexico's capital, as I was heading further south to Puebla, then on to the coast. Faced with this enormous, overwhelming city and limited time to discover as much about the food as possible, I decided that there was only one way forward. My plan was to try as many different dishes, taste combinations, and ingredients as possible. In just over 24 hours I barely slept, instead opting to eat on average every 30–45 minutes. So much of it was so delicious that I wanted to finish everything that had been put in front of me. This soon became impossible, but undaunted I pressed on. After many hours, stall vendors had begun to look at me in despair. I am sure they were wondering exactly who this guy was who ordered enough food for three or four people, sat there tasting, and writing notes, then tipped heavily and left, to be seen crossing the road and taking a stool at the next stall. Mexico as a whole is famed for its street food, and it is hugely popular with all manner of residents; businessmen and bankers can be seen eating alongside manual workers and students. Good food is essential to Mexicans, and there is enormous variety because virtually everything is available in one form or another from a street stall, café, or market. Some recipes have remained unchanged for hundreds, and in some cases thousands, of years.

Day 31: Salvador de Bahia, Brazil With so many cultures coexisting in Brazil, the food cannot help but be influenced by Brazil's ethnic diversity, although each region's cuisine remains quite loyally distinct. In Salvador de Bahia, the food and the culture are dominated by the heritage of its many African inhabitants, descendants of the thousands of slaves brought to Brazil by the Portuguese to work the plantations. In fact, the state of Bahia has the largest African population outside of the African continent. Here, every side dish, street food snack, or piece of grilled fish is served with a fiery chili salsa made with cilantro, tomato, onion, and vinegar—and, of course, the hot little pods themselves. I've always been completely addicted to chilies and salsa. I asked my wife on our first date if she liked them because I honestly didn't think I could go out with someone who didn't. Luckily for us both, she does! In Salvador de Bahia, however, even I had to proceed with caution. I came across a lethal little round purple chili in a market. When I nibbled it—much to the amusement of the stall holder— it made my face go numb and I thought all of my teeth were going to fall out.

Caldo de sururu Spicy mussel soup

Serves 4–6

2 small fresh red-hot chilies, seeded and
finely chopped

2 garlic cloves

6 fresh cilantro sprigs, leaves removed and
stems finely chopped

2 tbsp olive oil

2 medium white onions, finely chopped

4½lb (2kg) mussels in their shells

6 ripe tomatoes, coarsely chopped

2 bay leaves

1¼ cups canned coconut cream or
coconut milk

juice of 2 limes plus extra limes, cut into
wedges, for garnish

sea salt and freshly ground black pepper

In the northeast of Brazil,
in the state of Bahia,
mussels are known as
"sururu." This is a great
soup to serve at the
beginning of a meal.
In Brazil it is served in
small cups or shot glasses,
and in many little cafés
it can be found served
alongside a cold glass
of beer. For a crunchy
addition, chopped roasted
peanuts can be mixed
through the soup.

1 Using a mortar and pestle, crush the chilies with the garlic and salt. Add the cilantro stems and work into a paste. Heat a large heavy pan over medium-high heat. Cook the chili paste in the oil. Add the onion and cook for 3 minutes or until softened. Tap each mussel lightly on the work surface, and discard any that do not open, then add the mussels, tomato, and 2 cups water to the onion mixture. Cover and cook for 3 minutes. Add the bay leaves and continue cooking until the mussels open (discard any unopened mussels). Remove from the heat, and transfer the mussels and onion to a bowl. Let cool. Strain the cooking liquid through a sieve and set aside.

2 Prize open the mussels completely; remove the meat and discard the shells. Place two-thirds of the mussel meat in a food processor with the cooled tomato and onion mixture. Purée with the coconut cream until smooth. Return the purée to the heavy pan with the strained mussel cooking liquid and another 2 cups water, bring to a boil, then reduce the heat and simmer for 10 minutes. Add the reserved whole mussels to the pan, season well with salt and pepper, and add the lime juice.

3 Taste the soup. It should be rich and creamy, with a good base of chili flavor. The lime juice cuts through the richness to ensure the soup has a perfect balance of flavors, rather than being cloying. Serve hot in small cups or shot glasses, with each serving garnished with a lime wedge.

Queijo na brasa Grilled salty cheese marinated with oregano

Makes 12 skewers

2 small dried red chilies, crushed

1 tbsp dried oregano or marjoram, crumbled

3 tbsp olive oil

juice of ½ lemon

1lb (450g) *queijo de coalho* or haloumi cheese, cut into 12 rectangular blocks

freshly ground black pepper

1   Crush the chilies with half the oregano, and mix with the olive oil and lemon juice. Set aside.

2   Thread the cheese onto 12 bamboo skewers, and soak the cheese, skewers and all, in cold water for an hour, to prevent the skewers burning on the grill and to remove excess salt from the cheese.

3   Heat a charcoal grill until the coals are white hot. (If you want to cook inside, heat a grill pan until very hot.) When your grill is ready, sprinkle the cheese skewers with the remaining oregano and a few grindings of black pepper. Grill the cheese for 2–3 minutes on each side until golden brown but still firm (not completely melted).

4   Arrange on a plate and drizzle with the chili-olive oil dressing. Serve at once. These skewers are delicious as a snack or could be eaten at the start of a summer barbecue before other dishes are served. They work very well for meat eaters and vegetarians alike because they are quite substantial and make a nice change from grilled corn on the cob.

In Bahia, street food can easily be redefined as beach food. There are scores of little cafés and stalls where things are freshly made for lounging customers. Teenage boys and girls run around taking orders up and down the white sandy beach and ferrying them back to the cafés. There are also vendors who walk along selling their wares. It was from one of these that I had these fantastic skewers, fresh from a charcoal-filled brazier. When the smoky grilled cheese is handed over, it comes with a wad of paper towels and a warning in Portuguese that it is very hot. I take heed.

Acaraje com salada fresca Bean patties with avocado and tomato salad

Serves 4–6

These bean patties are extremely tasty, especially in combination with their usual accompaniment of salt-dried prawns and a zingy fresh salad. Street vendors often serve the acaraje split and filled with a prawn purée known as "vatapá," or in a vegetarian version with a tomato and chili salsa, and they are traditionally cooked in palm oil. Stalls selling acaraje are found everywhere in Salvador de Bahia. Acaraje is an evening dish, enjoyed before you go on to a party—something at which the Brazilians excel.

For the acaraje

2¼lb (1kg) dried black-eyed peas

1 large onion, grated

1 tsp cayenne pepper

2 garlic cloves, finely chopped

2in (5cm) piece of fresh ginger, grated

1 fresh hot red chili, seeded and
    finely chopped

vegetable oil for frying

sea salt and freshly ground black pepper

For the salad

1 avocado, sliced

4 ripe tomatoes, sliced

4 scallions (green onions), sliced

2 fresh green jalapeño or serrano chilies,
    seeded and finely chopped

juice of 1 lemon

1 tbsp vinegar

2 tbsp good-quality olive oil

1 Soak the peas in cold water for 2 hours. Rinse well in fresh cold water, and remove the skins and black eyes. Put the peas and onion in a pan. Cover with water, bring to a boil, and simmer for about 40 minutes until soft. Drain. Purée the mixture and cayenne pepper in a food processor until smooth.

2 Heat a little oil in a heavy frying pan. Cook the garlic and ginger over low heat for 2 minutes until fragrant. Add the paste, season with salt and pepper, and keep over low heat. Beat the mixture well with a wooden spoon to prevent it from sticking, as you would when making polenta. Cook for 15–20 minutes, stirring from the bottom occasionally. Check seasoning. Remove from the heat and set aside.

3 Heat oil in a heavy pan over medium-high heat. When hot, take a dessert spoon and quickly dip it into the hot oil. Fill the spoon with the black-eyed pea mixture, forming a firm, round shape. Place in the hot oil. Continue until you have a few patties in the pan. Cook for 6–8 minutes or until golden brown. Drain on paper towels. Continue cooking in small batches until all the mixture is used.

4 To make the salad, mix together the avocado, tomato, scallions, and chilies. Combine the lemon juice, vinegar, and olive oil and season well with salt and pepper. Pour this dressing over the salad, and serve with the fried acaraje and perhaps some grilled prawns.

Barbecued jerk chicken with pineapple salsa

Serves 4

4 boneless chicken breast halves

4 tbsp jerk paste (see below)

For the jerk paste

5 jalapeño chilies, seeded and
  finely chopped

2 tbsp ground allspice

1 tbsp ground cinnamon

1 tbsp ground nutmeg

juice of 3 limes

1 onion, finely chopped

finely grated zest of 2 oranges

½ tbsp tamarind paste (see p30)

For the pineapple salsa

¼ fresh pineapple, peeled and
  cut into ½in (1cm) dice

1 crisp green apple, cored and diced

½ bunch of fresh cilantro

1 fresh red jalapeño or serrano chili, seeded
  and diced

juice of 2 limes

1 small red onion, diced

pinch of sea salt

freshly ground black pepper

In Jamaica, jerk paste is traditionally used to marinate barbecued chicken or pork. The recipe here uses chicken breast, but chicken pieces such as drumsticks and thighs work just as well, as do pork ribs. The secret to success is in the marinating: the longer the better. The blend of spices is so invigorating to the taste buds it's quite addictive—no fingers in the jar now! The smell of the meat when it is cooking is evocative of the finished product. When it is done, it will surely be eaten at once. The pineapple salsa supplies a fresh, zingy flavor that complements the fiery paste.

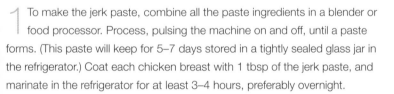

1 To make the jerk paste, combine all the paste ingredients in a blender or food processor. Process, pulsing the machine on and off, until a paste forms. (This paste will keep for 5–7 days stored in a tightly sealed glass jar in the refrigerator.) Coat each chicken breast with 1 tbsp of the jerk paste, and marinate in the refrigerator for at least 3–4 hours, preferably overnight.

2 When you are ready to cook, prepare the pineapple salsa by combining all the ingredients in a medium bowl. Set aside until ready to use.

3 Heat an outdoor grill until hot. Grill the chicken on both sides until white throughout but still juicy. Serve with the pineapple salsa. (For variation, serve with the peach salsa on pp94–95.)

Salsa de melocotón
Fresh peach salsa

This is a juicy salsa, spiked by the chilies and spices, and it works well as an accompaniment to grilled meat or barbecued chicken. In Mexico, from where it originates, it is usually served with goat; however, it works equally well with lamb, chicken, or pork. You could use a crisp apple such as a Pink Lady or Braeburn in place of the peaches or nectarines. Or perhaps even make it as a tomato salsa instead.

Serves 8

1 garlic clove, finely chopped

3 medium-hot fresh red jalapeño chilies, seeded and finely chopped

3 scallions (green onions), thinly sliced

½ red onion, finely diced

3 fresh ripe peaches or nectarines

juice of 3 limes

½ tsp pimentón (good-quality paprika)

pinch of sea salt

freshly ground black pepper

1 Place the garlic, chilies, scallions, and red onion in a bowl. Slice the peaches in half but do not peel. Remove the pits and cut the flesh into ½in (1cm) dice. Add to the bowl. Pour in the lime juice (this helps to prevent the peach from discoloring, as well as adding a bit of zing).

2 Add the pimentón and salt to the salsa, and season with pepper. Gently stir until well mixed. Serve as an accompaniment to grilled meat or chicken.

Lezumes en escabeche
Spicy vegetable pickle

Makes 1 large glass jar

¼ cup rice wine vinegar

¼ cup red wine vinegar

1 tbsp sugar

2 tsp sea salt

3 dried allspice berries

2 bay leaves

6 onions, finely chopped, rinsed in cold
water, and drained

2 carrots, finely chopped

1 red bell pepper, seeded and
finely chopped

4 fresh red jalapeño or serrano chilies,
seeded and finely chopped

fresh cilantro, mint, or flat-leaf parsley,
finely chopped

This brilliant pickled sauce from Mexico is usually served with tamales, tacos, and empanadas. It is best to make a large amount, as it will keep for many weeks in the refrigerator.

1 Bring the rice wine vinegar, red wine vinegar, sugar, salt, allspice, and bay leaves to a simmer in a covered heavy saucepan over medium-high heat, then remove the pan from the heat.

2 Pack the onion, carrot, red pepper, and chilies into a large sterilized glass jar or container with a secure-fitting lid, and pour the vinegar mixture over the top. Let cool at least 4 hours before using. (The pico de gallo will keep for a long time, but must be refrigerated once opened.)

3 Before using, mix the vegetable pickle with the chopped fresh herbs. Serve as an accompaniment to grilled or roasted meat, or the Seafood Empanadas on pp102–103.

Bistec con chimichurri
Seared steak with chimichurri

Serves 6

6 tender beef steaks, the cut of your choice

a little good-quality olive oil

salt and freshly ground black pepper

For the chimichurri

3 small dried red chilies

3 garlic cloves, peeled

1 tsp sea salt

½ tsp sugar

¼ cup vinegar

juice of 2 lemons

½ cup olive oil

½ bunch flat-leaf parsley,
  coarsely chopped

30 fresh oregano or marjoram
  leaves, coarsely chopped

1 To make the chimichurri, crush the dried chilies using a pestle and mortar. Add the garlic, salt, and sugar, and continue pounding until you have a smooth paste. (The salt and sugar will act as abrasives and help form a paste.) Next add the vinegar and lemon juice to moisten the paste, then mix in the olive oil. Sprinkle in the parsley and oregano, and season with pepper. Taste the sauce and adjust the seasoning if necessary. It should have a bold mix of flavors, to bring out the sweetness of the beef.

2 Heat a little olive oil in a heavy frying pan over medium heat. Working in batches as needed, when the pan is hot, sear the steaks on both sides until cooked to the desired doneness. Transfer to a large pan or platter and let rest for a few minutes. Pour any meat juices that have collected in the pan into the chimichurri. Transfer to serving plates, top each steak with chimichurri, and serve at once. Alternatively, grill the beef instead of pan-searing, or use pork chops or grilled chorizo sausages instead.

Chimichurri is a spectacularly good sauce that is used throughout Argentina, and it is an ever-popular accompaniment to the beef for which that country is famed. It has a very memorable and unique taste that is spicy hot, salty, and sour all at once. I first had it in a market in Buenos Aires, where it was liberally splashed over a grilled chorizo roll. Chimichurri completely transforms any dish of grilled meat or chicken— it's brilliant.

Picarones
Sweet potato and pumpkin doughnuts

These anise seed-infused pumpkin and sweet potato doughnuts are deliciously addictive and very easy to make. Picarones are a popular snack all over Ecuador and Peru, and are traditionally accompanied by "chancaca," a sugarcane syrup. They work very well served piping hot with honey or sugar syrup, or even maple syrup if you prefer. The sweetness of the sweet potato and pumpkin combines beautifully with the spices, black pepper, and salt, topped off with a drizzle of golden honey.

Makes 12–15 doughnuts

2 medium sweet potatoes, about 9–10oz (250–275g) total, peeled and cut into large chunks

½lb (250g) pumpkin or butternut squash, peeled and cut into large chunks

1 tsp salt

½ tsp crushed anise seed

2 cups all-purpose flour

1 envelope (¼oz) active dry yeast

freshly ground black pepper

oil for deep frying

honey or maple syrup to serve

1 Place the sweet potato and pumpkin in a large saucepan with just enough water to soften (don't add too much water, as the sweet potato and pumpkin have enough liquid content of their own—otherwise you will end up with mush). Bring to a boil and simmer until tender, stirring frequently, to prevent sticking.

2 Drain off any excess liquid, and mash the sweet potato and pumpkin together to form a smooth purée. Season with the salt, anise seed, and pepper. Transfer to a large bowl, then stir in the flour. In a small bowl, sprinkle the yeast over ¼ cup warm water and stir to mix. Set aside for 5–10 minutes until the yeast bubbles. Add to the sweet potato mixture to make a fairly firm dough, adding more water or flour if necessary. Cover and let sit for 2 hours in a warm, draft-free spot until the dough has puffed up to almost double in size.

3 Heat the oil for deep frying. To test if the oil is hot enough, tear off a small ball of dough and shape into a ring by pressing it flat in your hands and making a hole in the center with your thumb and forefinger. Gently drop the doughnut into the oil, being careful to avoid any splattering from the hot oil, and fry until golden brown on both sides, turning once during the cooking. Drain on paper towels. Taste and adjust the seasoning of the dough—it may need a little extra salt or some more anise seed. When you are happy with the seasoning, form the rest of the dough into rings, and fry in batches until pale golden brown on both sides, again turning once during cooking.

4 These are best eaten at once. Serve piping hot with honey or maple syrup for drizzling over the top.

Sopa mexicana de flor de calabaza
Mexican pumpkin flower soup

squash flowers such as pumpkin and courgette are found in many recipes across South America. They are delicious, particularly when lightly cooked. In Spain, France, and Italy they crop up in all sorts of recipes. It was fascinating to see them so frequently used around Mexico on all kinds of street stalls and in little cafés, where they would have been appearing in similar recipes for hundreds of years. This fresh summer soup with many of the exciting characteristics of Mexican street food is spiked with a tantalizing edge of green chili and lime juice.

Serves 6

3½ cups good-quality chicken stock

a little olive oil

2 fresh green jalapeño or serrano chilies, seeded and finely chopped

2 garlic cloves, finely chopped

1 onion, finely chopped

2 ripe tomatoes

8oz (225g) pumpkin flowers or zucchini flowers

juice of 2 limes

salt and freshly ground black pepper

1 Bring the chicken stock to a boil in a saucepan. Meanwhile, heat a large heavy frying pan and add a little olive oil. Reserve some of the chilies to garnish the soup, and cook the remainder in the hot oil with the garlic for 1–2 minutes or until fragrant. Add the onion and cook, stirring occasionally, until pale golden brown.

2 Cut the tomatoes in half, and grate the open side of each half on a large grater. (This is a quick method of getting the pulp from the tomatoes; the skin stays in your hand and can then be discarded.) Add the tomato to the pan with the onion. Discard the stems from the pumpkin flowers and coarsely chop the flowers, reserving 6 whole flowers for garnish. When the tomato has cooked down slightly, add the chopped pumpkin flowers to the pan. Cook for 2 minutes until the flowers are barely wilted. Pour in the hot chicken stock, and season with salt and pepper. Simmer for 5 minutes.

3 While the soup is simmering, heat a small frying pan and add a little olive oil. Cook the reserved whole pumpkin flowers until they are wilted and parts are golden brown. Season with salt and pepper, and add the reserved green chilies. Remove from the heat and set aside.

4 Using a blender or food processor and working in batches as needed, process the soup until smooth; return it to the pan. Add the lime juice. Taste and adjust the seasoning—there should be a balance between the sweet onion, chicken stock, spicy green chilies, and salt. The lime juice wakes up the flavors and provides a delicious sour edge to this simple soup. To serve, pour into bowls and garnish each with a whole pumpkin flower and some green chilies.

Empanadas de marisco
Seafood empanadas

Makes 12

olive oil for cooking

2 white onions, finely chopped

2 garlic cloves, finely chopped

2 fresh green jalapeño or serrano chilies,
   seeded and finely chopped

½lb (225g) mussels in their shells

splash of white wine

¼lb (115g) peeled uncooked prawns

½lb (225g) white fish such as hake or cod

3 tomatoes, diced

juice of ½ lemon

½ bunch of cilantro, coarsely chopped

1 cup grated mild Cheddar cheese

sea salt and freshly ground black pepper

For the pastry

1¼ cups all-purpose flour

1 cup yellow masa harina

1 tsp baking powder

1 tsp salt

1 stick (4oz) unsalted butter, melted

2 large eggs

Empanadas can be large or small. These are about the size of a Cornish pasty—a substantial snack. The small ones, which are called empanaditas, are great because they consist of about three bites. After which, you can then help yourself to a second or third empanadita! Seafood empanadas are a particular speciality in Ecuador, Argentina, and Chile. Remember, you must be careful with mussels. Before you use them, tap each one lightly on a work surface and discard those that do not close. Once cooked, discard any that remain unopened.

1 Heat a little oil in a heavy frying pan over medium-high heat. Cook the onion, garlic, and chilies until soft. Remove from the pan. Add the mussels and a splash of white wine to the pan, and cover. Steam for 3 minutes or until the mussels open. Remove the mussels from the pan, discard the shells, and set the meat aside. Strain the cooking liquid through a fine sieve and return to a clean pan.

2 Add the prawns, fish, tomato, and onion mixture to the cooking liquid. Simmer gently for about 4 minutes. Season with salt and pepper, and add the lemon juice. Remove the solids with a slotted spoon, and add to the mussels. Simmer the cooking liquid until reduced by one-third. Pour over the seafood, and add the cilantro and grated cheese. Season to taste and set aside.

3 Sift the flour, masa harina, baking powder, and salt into a large bowl. Stir in the cooled melted butter. Whisk ⅓ cup water and 1 of the eggs in a small bowl. Add to the flour mixture. Knead for 2 minutes until smooth and pliable.

4 Preheat the oven to 400°F (200°C). On a floured surface, roll out the dough until 1in (2.5cm) thick. Cut into 2–2½in (5–6cm) rounds. Place a spoonful of the seafood mixture just below the center of each round. Brush the edge of the pastry with egg wash, then fold the top half over, to form a half-moon. Crimp the edges together, squeezing out any air. Bake for 12–15 minutes until golden.

Salsa verde Green tomato salsa

Serves 6

6 (unripe) green tomatoes

1 onion

2 garlic cloves

4 fresh green jalapeño or serrano chilies,
   seeded and finely chopped

½ bunch cilantro leaves, coarsely chopped

2 avocados

½ bunch parsley, coarsely chopped

juice of 2 limes

2 tbsp olive oil

salt and freshly ground black pepper

In Mexico, the two most popular sauces that can accompany just about every dish are salsa roja and salsa verde. There might be only two names for the sauces, but there are hundreds of recipes that vary from stall to stall. Both the red sauce and the green are vibrantly colored and packed full of flavor, and are great on a filled taco or tortilla. Salsa verde was my favorite of all the sauces that I tasted in Mexico City. You can alter the proportions of the ingredients to suit your taste. If green tomatoes are not available, choose the least-ripe tomatoes that you can find, for sourness.

1 Cut the tomatoes in half. Scoop out the center core of seeds and place in a sieve over a bowl. Chop the flesh into a fine dice and set aside. Cut the onion in half, and grate the flesh so that you are left with a pulp. Set this aside also.

2 Cut the garlic in half and remove any green shoot from the center (this part of the garlic is bitter and can cause digestive problems). Chop the garlic finely. Using a large pestle and mortar, pound the garlic with the green chilies and a pinch of salt to make a smooth paste. Add half of the cilantro leaves and all of the onion to the paste. Still using the pestle and mortar, continue to pound until you have a coarse green paste.

3 Using a wooden spoon, push the tomato cores and their seeds through the sieve into the pestle and mortar, extracting all the juice. Discard the seeds and pour any juice that has collected in the bowl into the paste.

4 Halve, peel, and pit the avocado. Cut the flesh into ½in (1cm) dice. Add the avocado and green tomato to the paste. Pound a few times so part of it is crushed and the remaining part remains as dice. Mix in the parsley and remaining cilantro. Mix in the lime juice and olive oil. Season well with salt and pepper. Check the seasoning. The avocado makes it sweet, the lime juice and green tomato add the sour element, and the green chilies and black pepper supply heat. The salsa should have a real tang and zip to it. Adjust the green chili content to suit your taste, if necessary.

5 Serve in a bowl or in a sandwich, or spread on steak, grilled lamb, grilled chorizo, or sausages. It is great with just about anything.

Mole pipian Pipian sauce with cinnamon

Serves 8

3 tbsp olive oil

2 dried red chilies

1 onion, finely chopped

2 garlic cloves, finely chopped

1 cup shelled raw peanuts

1 cup hulled raw pumpkin seeds (pepitas)

3 cloves

½ tsp ground allspice

½ tsp ground cinnamon

½ tsp dried thyme

1 canned chipotle (smoked jalapeño chili) in adobo sauce

1 tsp sugar

2½ cups chicken stock

juice of 1 lime

sea salt and freshly ground black pepper

Moles are an integral complex part of Mexican culinary heritage. Areas such as Puebla are famous for them. They date back many centuries, and there are many different types. Some blend chocolate with chili, which dates back to Aztec times. There are often scores of ingredients blended to a smooth paste. I tasted one version that was a combination of nuts and seeds, and different types of chilies.

1 Heat the olive oil in a large frying pan. Add the dried chilies and cook for a minute, turning, until toasted. Transfer the chilies to a bowl, cover with hot water, and soak for 20 minutes. When soft, cut off and discard the chili stem. Discard some or all of the chili seeds, if desired. In the same pan, cook the onion and the garlic, stirring occasionally until softened, adding a little extra oil if needed.

2 In a separate pan over low heat, first toast the peanuts, then the pumpkin seeds, watching carefully to make sure that they don't burn. Transfer the peanuts and pumpkin seeds to a food processor, and add the onion/garlic mixture, soaked chilies, cloves, allspice, cinnamon, thyme, chipotle, and sugar. Process with ½ cup of the chicken stock until smooth, working in small batches, if necessary.

3 Return the purée to the pan in which the onion was cooked and cook over low heat. Add the remaining chicken stock, and stir until the sauce is the texture of melted ice cream. Taste the sauce. There is a sweetness from the onion and chicken stock, and the chilies and spices are hot. The roasted nuts and salt add to its savory qualities. Adjust the seasoning, if necessary.

4 Add the lime juice just before serving, to wake up the flavors and bring them into balance. Serve with grilled or roasted meat.

Molho de cajú Green cashew nut sauce

Serves 8 or more

4 tbsp raw cashews

2 garlic cloves

2 fresh green jalapeño or serrano chilies,
  seeded and diced

2 shallots, finely diced

½ cup olive oil or untoasted sesame oil

1 tbsp white wine vinegar

juice of 2 limes

½ bunch of fresh basil, coarsely chopped

½ bunch of cilantro, coarsely chopped

pinch of sea salt

freshly ground black pepper

pinch of sugar or a little freshly
  squeezed orange juice (optional)

1 Dry-roast the cashews over medium heat, watching carefully to avoid burning, and turning frequently until they are golden brown all over.

2 To make the sauce, first make a paste of the garlic and chilies in a food processor or blender, then add the shallot and process until a coarse paste forms. Now add the cooled cashews, and process once again until smooth. With the motor running, very gradually add the oil in a thin, steady stream, then add the vinegar and 1 tbsp water. With the motor on a low speed, add the lime juice, then the basil and cilantro, until you have a smooth green paste. Taste and adjust the seasoning with a pinch of sea salt and black pepper, and more lime juice if needed. If the chilies are too hot, add a pinch of sugar or some orange juice, if you like.

This is a lovely creamy marinade for chicken, beef, or prawns—or anything else that you may be cooking on the grill. Alternatively, the sauce can be used to coat the meat once it is cooked (and still hot). It also makes a tasty dipping sauce and can be served in a small bowl as an accompaniment to a summer barbecue, perhaps with crudités or some fresh crusty bread.

Pudim de abóbora Pumpkin pudding

Serves 4–6

1½lb (675g) pumpkin (choose a sweet,
  firm-fleshed variety) or butternut squash,
  peeled and cut into cubes

4 large eggs

½ cup (packed) plus 2 tbsp brown sugar

½ tsp ground cloves

½ tsp ground nutmeg

½ tsp ground cinnamon

½ tsp ground ginger

½ tsp salt

1 cup half-and-half or light cream

butter to grease the mold

1 Preheat the oven to 350°F (180°C). Combine the pumpkin in a large saucepan with a little water, and cook over medium heat until soft. Drain, then mash until smooth, removing any stringy bits.

2 Beat the eggs with half the brown sugar until pale and thick. Add the remaining sugar, the spices, and the salt. Mix the half-and-half into the pumpkin purée, then fold in the egg mixture.

3 Lightly butter 6 individual ramekins or custard cups. Alternatively, to make one large pudding, butter 1–1¼ quart soufflé dish or other baking dish. Set the ramekins (or large dish) in a roasting pan and carefully fill the pan with enough hot water to reach about halfway up the sides of the ramekins (or large dish). Carefully place in the oven, and bake until just set or a toothpick comes out clean—about 40 minutes for individual ramekins and 1 hour 20 minutes for a large single pudding. Serve warm with biscotti or similar cookies.

Sweet pumpkin desserts are very common across South America, and they vary enormously. This recipe came from a small stall in Rio. It has a light creamy texture like a crème brûlée. The delicious combination of brown sugar and the selection of spices makes it very interesting. It should be eaten with little nut biscotti or cookies, and accompanied by an espresso or iced coffee to complete the picture. The Brazilian stall holder was only too pleased to help me with this recipe, offering me more hot pudding and coffee at the same time. It could also be quite easily made into a tart with a pastry crust.

Southern Europe

The enjoyment of good food is an integral part of life across Southern Europe. By extension, street food is regarded as more than a way to fuel the body. It is a celebration of strong traditions, with some recipes being handed down over centuries and providing a culinary identity for these countries, as beloved as the bacon sandwich in Britain or the hamburger in the United States. Religion and the festivals that accompany it play a strong role in these cuisines, with some dishes appearing only on particular feasts, saints' days, or religious holidays. There are samplings from Southern Italy, Sicily, Malta, and Spain. The recipes are varied, unusual, and not-your-average fare—a delicious demonstration of these cuisines.

Day 46: Catania, Sicily On the first day of my stay in Catania, I was walking through a rundown area of the city on a cold, crisp day in February. The majority of the small rough-looking businesses were either motorcycle repair shops or butchers specializing in horsemeat. From a distance, I spied a jewel of a stall on the street corner. Plumes of blue smoke could be seen as I walked down the hill towards it, following the scent like a hound. It was not until I was right there that I saw about 50 small purple artichokes had been grilled in the charcoal, and nestled among the hot coals. They shone out as something delicious on this otherwise dilapidated industrial street. I paid for a couple and got change for a euro. They were anointed with some thick green olive oil, and I was handed a couple of napkins from the pocket of the stall vendor. He took another drag of his cigarette and resumed chatting with his two friends while turning some red peppers. I stood by the stall and started to peel the most burnt leaves from the outside, dropping them into a cardboard box on the pavement. The inside was delicious and filled with vibrant green stuffing. Oil oozed out and ran down my wrist, but I didn't really care, as I stood by the charcoal fire eating some of the most delicious morsels that I can remember.

Day 48: Catania, Sicily I was walking toward the train station on my way to Palermo, the island's main city. My bags were heavy and it was cold, but I had heard that there were good examples of street food and typical regional snacks around this part of town. Pretty soon I found such a place, and the food inside was definitely worth the hardship. The dingy interior was taken up by a large open-fronted wood oven. Across the oven were four or so long metal spits with small baby chickens roasting in front of the fire. On the floor of the oven was a large pan of hand-cut potatoes, catching all the juices dripping from the chickens being idly turned by the barrel-chested owner. Family members were leaning over the wooden counter, watching a loud Italian quiz show on a mounted television in the corner of the room—a familiar sight found in fast-food restaurants, cafés, and takeaway shops the world over. The big difference was that the food being served was exceptionally fresh and tasty. I was hardly able to wait patiently. I ordered my half chicken, and it was wrapped in foil with some potatoes. I eagerly took it outside, found a sunlit square, and sat on a stone bench to enjoy the crisp, juicy roast chicken with its generous onion, olive, rosemary, and chili stuffing (see pp120–121).

Crispeddi Semolina flour fritters

Serves 6–8

2 small cakes (0.6oz each) fresh yeast

1 cup hot water (about 110°F/43°C)

4–5½ cups semolina flour

¾ cup fresh ricotta

4 salt-packed anchovies, chopped

1 tbsp salt-packed capers, rinsed, drained,
  squeezed dry, and chopped

1 tsp chopped fennel fronds or
  ½ tsp crushed fennel seeds

pinch of sea salt

pinch of sugar

light olive oil for deep frying

freshly ground black pepper

1 Mix the yeast with a little of the hot water to make a paste. Put the semolina flour in a large bowl. Make a well in the center, add the yeast paste and the remaining hot water, and whisk to make a batter. Let rise in a warm, draft-free spot for 2 hours, as you would with bread dough.

2 Mix the ricotta with the anchovy and capers. Add lots of black pepper and the fennel, salt, and sugar. Roll the ricotta mixture into balls about ¾in (2cm) in diameter. Use a little oil on your hands so that they do not stick. Heat the oil in a heavy pan over medium-high heat. Dip the balls into the batter and, using a spoon, drop very gently into the pan to avoid splattering. Cook for 4–5 minutes or until golden brown on all sides. Drain on paper towels and serve at once.

Panelle (chickpea fritters) This much-loved snack is often served sandwiched in a ciabatta roll. It is best eaten piping hot and fresh from the oven. Mix 3¾ cups chickpea flour with a pinch of salt, 2 tbsp olive oil, and 5½ cups water in a heavy saucepan. Cook over medium heat, stirring continuously with a wooden spoon, to prevent the mixture from sticking. Continue cooking for 20 minutes, or until the mixture starts to pull away from the edges. Season with salt and black pepper. Line a bread pan with plastic wrap. Pour the batter into the pan, and cover the surface with another layer of plastic wrap. Let sit until firm, at least 2 hours. Heat a baking sheet in the oven at 400°F (200°C). Turn out the loaf onto a work surface and cut into thin slices. Remove the baking sheet from the oven, and add a splash of olive oil. Place the slices on the tray, and return to the oven. Check after 4 minutes and, when the slices are golden brown, turn over to brown on the other side. Serve at once with freshly grated Parmesan, coarsely chopped flat-leaf parsley, some lemon wedges, and a few grindings of black pepper.

These snacks are eaten on market days or the saint's day of a town or village. They are perfect to be shared among friends and are great with drinks to start an evening. Sun-dried tomatoes marinated in oregano and olive oil can be added to the ricotta mixture with or without the anchovies. Or try pieces of cooked bacon or coarsely chopped pitted olives instead. You can even omit the anchovies and simply use fresh herbs such as basil and parsley, or arugula.

Cipolle d'inverno e pancetta alla griglia Grilled scallions wrapped in pancetta

I had this deliciously simple and very tasty snack late at night when I was in Palermo in Sicily, where it was being grilled in a square near some late-night drinking haunts. Despite the freezing February weather, everyone was drinking and eating outside, with many people huddled around large barbecue grills where lots of tasty things were being cooked. The air was thick with the smoke and aromas of cooking food, and there were hungry partygoers hopping from foot to foot expectantly, waiting for their bread rolls to be removed from the grill.

Serves 8

24 scallions (green onions), trimmed
   and peeled
good-quality olive oil
16 thin pancetta slices
2 lemons, cut into wedges

crushed dried red chilies
a few fresh basil or arugula leaves (optional)
fresh Italian bread such as ciabatta or
   focaccia, or other crusty bread rolls
salt and freshly ground black pepper

1 Place the scallions in a bowl, and drizzle with a little olive oil. Season well with salt and pepper; toss to coat.

2 On a clean work surface, lay out two strips of pancetta side by side, with the long sides together. Repeat with all the pancetta, so that you have a bit of a production line. Place 3 scallions at one end of each of the pancetta strips, and roll the pancetta tightly around the scallions to cover. Grill on a preheated hot barbecue or grill pan, or under a hot broiler, for a couple of minutes on each side until golden and crispy. Transfer to a cutting board, and cut into small ¾in (2cm) chunks. (Cutting up the scallions makes them much easier to eat.)

3 Split open a crusty bread roll and put the scallion pieces inside. Drizzle with a little olive oil. Season with salt and pepper. Squeeze a little lemon juice over the top, and sprinkle with a few crushed chilies. Add a few basil or arugula leaves. Sandwich the filled roll together, and place on the barbecue or under the broiler for a couple of minutes each side so that it is toasted.

4 Eat at once, with your sleeves rolled up and lots of paper napkins on hand. This dish is ideal as part of a summer picnic or barbecue, or as a starter before the main meat or fish is grilled. Alternatively, chop the grilled scallion into pieces, pile on top of crostini, drizzle with a little olive oil, and sprinkle with chopped basil or arugula. Season with the lemon and crushed chilies, and eat with your fingers.

Pastizzi tar-rikotta
Savory ricotta-filled pastries

Makes 15–20

For the pastry

3½ cups all-purpose flour, sifted

½ tsp salt

½–⅔ cup (4½–5½oz) lard or butter

For the filling

1lb (450g) ricotta

3 eggs, beaten

salt and freshly ground black pepper

1 To make the pastry, mix the flour and salt with about 1 cup cold water in a bowl until it forms a soft, pliable but not sticky dough. Knead well, then let rest for about 1½ hours. Set the dough on a floured work surface and cut into 3 pieces. Roll each piece into a long rectangle about 1¾in (4cm) wide. Roll, stretch, and pull each one into long strips. Spread half the lard over the entire length of each strip of dough, first with a small metal spatula, then with clean, dry hands. Take one end of one strip of the dough and roll it up like a pinwheel (when rolling it up, do it unevenly—sometimes turning the dough tightly; sometimes more loosely). Repeat with the remaining two strips of dough. Rest the dough in the refrigerator for at least 30 minutes.

2 Take the rolled strips of dough out of the refrigerator and roll them flat again on a floured work surface. Spread with the remaining lard. Roll the strips like a pinwheel once again, this time in a different direction from the first roll—all this rolling enhances the flakiness of the finished pastry. Rest the pastry in the refrigerator for another 30 minutes.

3 Preheat the oven to 400°F (200°C). To make the filling, put the ricotta in a bowl and season with salt and pepper. Mash the ricotta with a fork, then add the beaten egg. Using a sharp knife, cut off pieces of dough ¾–1¼in (2–3cm) in diameter. Next, using your fingers and thumb, press down on each ball so that it is a thin flat disc. Put a tablespoon of the seasoned ricotta cheese mix in the middle of each circle. Fold each circle from the top and the bottom to the center, and squeeze the edges of the pastry together with your fingers to seal the pocket (the horizontal ends form into points). Place the pastizzi on a lightly oiled baking sheet, and bake in the oven for 20 minutes or until the pastry is golden and flaky.

In Malta, pastizzi are traditionally eaten for breakfast. They are a delicious and hearty way to start the day if you are setting off early. In fact, they are great at any time when eaten fresh from the oven. The most popular and cheapest Maltese street food, pastizzi can be bought from small shops and stalls called "pastizzeriji" which are spread around the island. The two main types are pastizzi "tar-rikotta" (cheese) and pastizzi "tal-pizelli" (peas). These rich diamond-shaped flaky pastries are best eaten hot, with lots of napkins.

Pollo con olive, cipolla e rosmarino ripieno Poussin stuffed with olives, onion, and rosemary

Spit-roasted chicken and potatoes in foil, eaten on a park bench in winter is one of my great memories from my trips to Sicily. I bought this fabulous takeaway dish from one of the many family-run eateries dotted around Catania. The hand-cut potatoes cooked in the juices dripping from the chickens added another dimension to the repast. There are lots of different flavors here, and the combination stimulates all the taste buds. It is very easy to increase the stuffing in order to make this dish serve more people.

Serves 4

4 onions, thinly sliced

3½oz (100g) black olives, pitted and
  coarsely chopped

5 fresh rosemary sprigs, chopped

4 garlic cloves, halved and any green inner
  shoot discarded

2 small dried red chilies, crushed

2 tbsp olive oil plus a little extra

juice of 1 lemon

4 poussins or baby chickens, about
  1lb 2oz (500g) each

salt and freshly ground black pepper

1 Preheat the oven 400°F (200°C). In a bowl, combine the onions, olives, and rosemary. Finely chop the garlic with the dried chilies. Add to the onion mixture with the 2 tbsp olive oil and the lemon juice. Mix well and season with salt and pepper. Stuff each chicken with a generous amount of the stuffing.

2 Heat a little oil in a heavy ovenproof frying pan over medium-high heat. Season the outside of the chickens with salt and pepper. Brown the chickens in the pan, turning once to brown on all sides. When browned, transfer the whole pan to the oven and roast for 30–35 minutes until the meat is tender, basting regularly with all the roasting juices. (If cooking a larger chicken, allow a longer cooking time—usually 1 hour to 1 hour 20 minutes or so.) To check, insert the tip of a small knife near the bone; if the juices run clear, the chicken is cooked.

3 Serve the chickens with piping-hot home-made french fries or roasted potatoes, or with a green salad with bitter and peppery leaves.

Note To try to be more authentic (but without using a spit or rotisserie), place a pan of hand-cut french fries splashed with a little olive oil and seasoned with salt and pepper at the bottom of the oven while you are cooking the chicken. Put the chicken on a rack above the potatoes, so that all the juices drip onto the potatoes. Turn the potatoes regularly during cooking, and pour any leftover juices from inside the chicken over the top just before serving.

Ravioli di Carnalivari Sweet fried ravioli

Serves 6

For the pasta
4 cups bread flour
6 tbsp sugar
pinch of sea salt
6 tbsp unsalted butter
1 egg yolk
1 tsp vanilla extract
¼ cup milk

For the filling
12oz (350g) fresh ricotta cheese
3½oz (100g) caster sugar

grated zest of 1 lemon
½ tsp ground cinnamon
1 tsp vanilla extract
1½oz (45g) bittersweet chocolate (at least
    70% cocoa solids), grated
2 tbsp candied orange and lemon
    peel, finely chopped
a little beaten egg yolk for brushing
about 1 cup light olive oil

confectioners' (powdered) sugar for dusting

These are really delicious, and the creamy filling is a treasure trove of unexpected flavors. I love things such as this where you have no idea what is waiting inside until you take your first bite. Pastries similar to these are made in Sicily, Sardinia, Malta, and across the Mediterranean.

1 To make the pasta, rub the flour, sugar, salt, and butter together until the texture of breadcrumbs. Mix in the egg yolk, vanilla, and milk to form a small ball of dough. Let rest for 30 minutes.

2 Meanwhile, mix together the ricotta, sugar, lemon zest, cinnamon, and vanilla until smooth. Stir in the chocolate and orange and lemon peel. Taste and adjust the flavors to your liking.

3 To finish the ravioli, roll out the pastry to about ¼in (½cm) thick. Using a biscuit cutter or small plate, cut into discs 4–5in (10–12cm) in diameter. Spoon the ricotta paste onto the bottom half of the disc, in a half-moon shape, leaving a small rim. Brush the rim with egg yolk. Fold the pastry over and, with a cupped hand, carefully squeeze any air bubbles out of the filling. Seal the edges tightly—otherwise the ravioli will open while cooking.

4 Heat the olive oil over medium-high heat. When hot, shallow-fry 2 or 3 pastries at a time in batches. Cook for 3–4 minutes until golden all over. Drain on paper towels. Let cool, then dust with confectioners' sugar and serve.

Variation For a different taste, substitute dried fruits such as figs and apricots for the candied peel. Or you could use roasted pistachio nuts, or perhaps a coffee and chocolate combination.

Triglie de scoglio

Pan-fried red mullet with preserved lemon, olives, and parsley

The key to cooking a delicate fish such as red mullet is its absolute freshness. I had this dish at a small outdoor café near Catania's fish market. There were only a few dishes on the menu, and most of the customers of the surrounding cafés were market traders and other local characters all enjoying red mullet, crusty bread, and local white wine. The proprietor was cooking the mullet in large fish-shaped black pans, with about 8 small fish in each one. This is an impressive dish, but is not complicated to make. The stuffing can also be used for chicken breasts.

Serves 4

2 lemons

3 tbsp rock salt

1 garlic clove, halved and any green inner
  shoot discarded

30 black olives, pitted and coarsely
  chopped

½–1 fresh red jalapeño or serrano chili,
  seeded and finely chopped

20 fresh basil leaves, coarsely chopped

20 flat-leaf parsley leaves, coarsely chopped

juice of 1 lemon

2 tbsp extra virgin olive oil

a little light olive oil

4 fresh red mullet or other small firm, lean
  fish, 9–14oz (250–400g) each, gutted,
  scaled, and cleaned

sea salt and freshly ground black pepper

1 To make the preserved lemon, put the lemons into a small, tight-fitting pan. Cover with water and add the rock salt. Place a small lid or saucer on top of the lemons to keep them submerged. Bring to a boil, and simmer until tender when pierced with the tip of a sharp knife, 8–10 minutes. Refresh under cold running water. When the lemons are cool, cut in half, remove all the flesh and pith, and discard. Using a thin sharp knife, trim the inside of the skin, removing any remaining traces of the bitter white pith. Finely chop the lemon skin and set aside.

2 Preheat the oven to 350°F (180°C). Using the back of a knife, crush the garlic with a little sea salt, until a smooth paste forms. Mix together the garlic, olives, chili, basil, parsley, and preserved lemon. Add the lemon juice and olive oil, and season with salt and pepper.

3 Take one of the red mullet and pat dry with paper towels. Stuff the cavity with some of the olive and lemon mixture. Repeat the process with the remaining mullet. Season the fish inside and out with salt and pepper. Heat a little oil in an frying pan over medium-high heat. Pan-fry the mullet for 3 minutes. Turn gently and cook the other side for 2 minutes. Transfer the mullet to a baking dish, and bake in the oven for 5 minutes or until cooked through. (Alternatively, either grill the fish or bake entirely in the oven.) Serve at once with some mixed greens or braised spinach. The smoky roasted mullet and the stuffing combine brilliantly.

Mustazzoli Honey and nut pastries

Serves 4–6

For the pastry

3 cups all-purpose flour

6–8 tbsp lard or unsalted butter

3¼ cup sugar

2 eggs

2–4 tbsp milk

For the filling

12oz (350g) assorted shelled nuts, such as
  fresh walnuts, almonds, and pine nuts

½ cup honey

2 tbsp all-purpose flour

grated zest of 1 orange

1 tsp almond extract

confectioners' (powdered) sugar for dusting

These nut pastries make a great snack with a cup of strong coffee, mint tea, or alongside a bowl of vanilla ice cream. Variations of this sort of pastry can be found all around the Mediterranean in any region where nuts are cultivated, from the islands of Sicily, Sardinia, and Malta, to Turkey, Lebanon, and all the way to Morocco.

1 To make the pastry dough, sift the flour into a bowl. Rub 6 tbsp of the lard into the flour between your fingers, until it resembles the texture of breadcrumbs. Mix in the sugar, then add the eggs and milk, mixing until you have a soft dough. Cover and refrigerate for at least 1 hour. Make the filling while the pastry dough is resting.

2 Heat the oven to 350°F (180°C). Place the nuts on a baking sheet, and roast for 3–5 minutes until golden brown all over, shaking halfway through to make sure they do not burn. Remove the nuts from the oven, and increase the oven temperature to 400°F (200°C).

3 In a small saucepan, combine the honey with ¼ cup water. Bring the liquid to a boil. Stir in the 2 tbsp flour, little by little, until you have a smooth paste. Add the orange zest and almond extract. Coarsely chop the toasted nuts and stir them in. Remove from the heat, and let cool completely.

4 To make the pastries, divide the dough into two equal pieces. Roll out one piece to form a rectangle approximately 2 x 4in (5 x 10cm) and ¼in (½cm) thick. Spoon half the nut mixture onto the long side of the pastry rectangles, and roll the pastry over a couple of times to make a long nut swirl. Repeat with the second half of the pastry. Use the remaining lard to grease a length of baking parchment as long as the pastry rolls. Place the baking parchment on a baking sheet, then place the rolls onto the baking parchment. Cut the rolls into small squares of roughly ¾in (2cm)—the shapes can be a little irregular. Bake in the oven for 15–20 minutes until golden. Remove from the oven and let cool. Dust the finished pastries with confectioners' sugar and serve.

These artichokes are perfect for a summer picnic or as a starter for a barbecue. In Catania where I had them, they were eaten on the street as a hearty snack. I was there in February and it was very cold. It probably seemed a lot colder because I didn't have enough of the right clothes to wear as my luggage had been lost, but these sweet, smoky morsels somehow made all my troubles recede. There is no polite way to eat these— simply roll up your sleeves and dig in. When you get to the heart, you can pretty much eat it in one or two mouthfuls.

Carciofi ripieni alla griglia

Grilled artichokes with garlic, chilies, and pine nuts

Serves 4–6

⅔ cup pine nuts

4 garlic cloves, halved and any green inner
   shoot removed

2 small dried red chilies

1 small bunch of flat-leaf parsley leaves,
   finely chopped

3 tbsp good-quality extra virgin olive
   oil plus extra for serving

juice of 2 lemons

18 baby artichokes (in season in spring and
   early summer)

salt and freshly ground black pepper

lemon wedges for serving

1 Heat a charcoal grill until the coals are white-hot. Toast the pine nuts in a dry frying pan over medium-high heat for 2–3 minutes until golden brown. Watch carefully as they burn very easily. Finely chop the garlic, and finely crush the dried chilies with a pinch of salt. Mix together the pine nuts, garlic, chilies, parsley, olive oil, and lemon juice. Season well with salt and pepper.

2 Take an artichoke and trim down the stem. Pull the leaves apart, without pulling them off. Work your way to the center of the artichoke. Using a teaspoon, remove the hairy choke by scraping in a circular motion. Take a tsp of pine nut mixture and push it down toward the base. Add another spoonful of filling and spread it among the central inner leaves. Repeat with the remaining artichokes. Season the inside of the artichokes with salt and pepper.

3 Carefully place the artichokes among the white-hot coals, keeping them upright. Grill for 8–10 minutes, turning occasionally and cooking in batches if necessary. To test whether they are cooked, hold an artichoke with a pair of tongs. Insert the tip of small sharp knife into the base just above the stem. It should be soft. If not, cook for a few more minutes. Remove from the heat. Cool slightly.

4 Have some extra virgin olive oil and the lemon wedges ready. Pull off and discard the blackened outside leaves. Pour a little extra virgin olive oil into the center and squeeze with lemon. Peel off and eat the inner leaves. The soft, pale center can be eaten in a couple of mouthfuls, stalks and all.

Croquetas de bacalao Salt cod croquettes

Serves 4–6

8oz (225g) salt cod, soaked in several
    changes of cold water in the refrigerator
    for 24 hours (or use skinless, boneless
    cod fillet)

2 cups milk

2 bay leaves

1 large, all-purpose potato, about 10oz
    (300g), peeled and cut into large chunks

1 shallot, peeled and finely grated

1 tbsp flour

1 bunch flat-leaf parsley, coarsely chopped

½ tsp pimentón or good-quality paprika

sunflower oil for deep frying

salt and freshly ground black pepper

tomato sauce or salsa for serving

Bacalao, or salt cod, is very popular across the Mediterranean, in Portugal, Spain, and Italy, where it can be found in a number of dishes. I sampled this particular version, delicious fresh-cooked croquettes, at a stall in a market in southern Spain. Drawn by the lovely aroma, I tracked my way around the stalls until I found the person who was responsible for these tasty snacks.

1 Drain the salt cod and rinse well. Place in a saucepan with the milk and bay leaves. Slowly bring to a boil, and simmer gently for 4–5 minutes. Using a slotted spoon, transfer the cod from the pan to a large bowl, then put the potato chunks into the same saucepan. Add water to cover if necessary, and simmer for 15–20 minutes or until tender.

2 Meanwhile, shred the cooked salt cod with your fingers, and add to a bowl with the shallot, flour, three-quarters of the parsley, and pimentón. Drain the potatoes well, and add to the cod mixture. Toss to mix. Use a potato masher to mash everything together; the mixture can be quite coarse. Taste and season with salt and pepper if necessary. The mixture should be salty and sweet, with a warmth from the pimentón and black pepper. Scoop out spoonfuls of the mixture, form roughly into bite-size oval shapes, and place on a floured baking sheet.

3 In a large, heavy saucepan, heat oil to a depth of about 1½in (3cm) over medium-high heat for 5 minutes until shimmering, or until a small amount of the croquette mixture turns golden in about 45 seconds. Working in batches as needed, carefully lower 6 croquettes into the oil, one by one, using a slotted spoon. As soon as they turn golden on all sides (3–4 minutes), remove with the slotted spoon and drain on paper towels, keeping them warm while you fry the remaining croquettes in the same manner. Serve at once with generous spoonfuls of tomato dipping sauce or salsa.

Quaglie marinate con salsa di capperi
Marinated quail with caper sauce

Serves 2–4 as a starter

2 quail

2 garlic cloves, finely chopped

1 small dried red chili, finely crushed

pinch of salt

finely grated zest and juice of 1 lemon

1 tbsp finely chopped fresh marjoram,
 thyme, or oregano leaves

1 tbsp red wine vinegar

1 tbsp honey

½ cup dry white wine

2 tbsp coarsely chopped flat-leaf parsley

2 tbsp pine nuts or blanched almonds,
 dry-roasted until pale golden

freshly ground black pepper

For the caper sauce

1 preserved lemon (see p124), chopped

1 tbsp salt-packed capers, rinsed, drained,
 squeezed dry, and chopped

2 tbsp coarsely chopped fresh marjoram
 or basil leaves

1 tbsp red wine vinegar

3 tbsp extra virgin olive oil

Sicilian food is fascinating because it often combines sweet flavors with sour, salty, and peppery hot elements. Honey and vinegar are commonly used in Sicilian dressings and marinades. I had this at a small country fair in Sicily. You could smell something good long before you got to the line by the large barbecue pit. A simple dish to make at home, even if there are a few different stages, it works well served on a bed of herbed couscous, bulgur wheat salad, or a pilaf of rice or pearl barley. Try it with partridge or baby chickens, or even as skewers of chicken breast.

1 Soak 4 bamboo skewers in cold water for at least 30 minutes. Place 1 quail breast-side down on a clean work surface. Using kitchen shears, carefully cut around and remove the triangular piece of the backbone with the wishbone attached. Use the side of a heavy knife to flatten the bird. Insert a bamboo skewer through a wing, then through the leg meat. Repeat on the other side so that the bird is pinned flat. Repeat this process with the other quail.

2 Mince the garlic and chili with a pinch of salt to make a paste. Combine with the remaining marinade ingredients except for the parsley and pine nuts in a shallow glass or ceramic dish. Add the quail and season with pepper. Marinate in the refrigerator, covered, for at least 2 hours. Combine all the ingredients for the caper sauce. Check the seasoning—it should be salty and sour.

3 Preheat the oven to 425°F (220°C). Heat an ovenproof grill pan until very hot. Remove the birds from the marinade, and season. Grill skin-side down for 3–4 minutes or until the skin is a deep, rich brown. Turn over and transfer the whole pan to the oven for 5 minutes. (The juices should run rose pink when a knife is inserted close to the leg bone.) Pour the remaining marinade into a small saucepan and reduce by half, for 3–4 minutes. Serve with the hot marinade poured over the birds, a spoonful of caper sauce, and a scattering of pine nuts and parsley over the top.

Cudduruni Sicilian focaccia-style bread

Makes 2 large breads or 8 smaller ones

For the biga
½ small cake (0.6oz) fresh yeast
½ cup warm water
1 cup bread flour

For the dough
1 small cake (0.6oz) fresh yeast

1 tsp sugar
1½ cups warm water
7 tbsp biga (see below)
3 tbsp olive oil
4 cups bread flour
1½ tsp salt

Italy has always been famous for its breads— they have a delicious aroma and a wonderful open, aerated texture. This is largely due to what is called "biga," a fresh yeast starter. In traditional bakeries, the starter is kept going for decades, handed down from one generation to another. Plan ahead and make your starter the day before. Cudduruni is similar to focaccia, and can have various toppings, or be filled like a calzone. It is also served more simply as rounds of dough, fried until golden on both sides, and sprinkled with salt.

1 To make the biga, or starter, crumble the yeast into the warm water and add the flour. Mix together until you have a thick batter. Cover with a damp cloth, and leave at room temperature to ferment for at least 6 hours or overnight. The biga may separate in this period of time; simply stir it back together. (To keep your biga going, feed with a bit of warm water and flour each day, and mix together, or simply mix in a small offcut from the fresh dough.)

2 To make the dough, mix the yeast and the sugar, and break up with a teaspoon until you have a smooth paste. Whisk this into the warm water with the biga and the olive oil. Sift the flour and salt into a bowl, and mix in the yeast liquid. Mix together until you form a dough. Turn onto a floured board, and knead vigorously for 12–15 minutes until the dough is shiny and elastic. It should be springy to the touch.

3 Lightly flour a bowl and place the ball of dough in it. Cover and leave in a warm place until it has doubled in size, about 1½ hours.

Two types of bread To make a simple loaf, flour a baking tray and shape the dough on the tray. Allow to prove for 10 minutes. Bake in a preheated 425°F (220°C) oven for 25–35 minutes until golden, depending on the size and depth of the loaf. It is ready when the loaf sounds hollow when tapped on the bottom. Alternatively, take pieces of dough about the size of tennis balls and flatten until ½in (1cm) thick. Heat a splash of olive oil in a heavy pan over medium-high heat. Cook the rounds one at a time for 2–3 minutes on one side until golden. Turn over and cook for 2 more minutes on the other side. Sprinkle with salt and drizzle with some extra virgin olive oil. Eat piping hot.

Calzone con tonne, broccoli e ricotta

Grilled tuna, sprouting broccoli,
and ricotta calzone

Makes 6 medium calzone

1 fresh tuna steak, about 10oz (300g), cut ¾in (2cm) thick	juice of 1 lemon
8oz (225g) purple sprouting broccoli, cut into equal-sized florets	2 small dried chilies
	2 garlic cloves, peeled
¼ cup good-quality olive oil	8oz (225g) ricotta cheese
30 fresh basil leaves, coarsely chopped	1 recipe cudduruni dough (see p134)
	salt and freshly ground black pepper

1 Preheat the oven to 400°–425°F (200°–220°C). Heat a charcoal grill or grill pan until very hot. Season the tuna well with salt and pepper, and add the olive oil. Grill for about 2 minutes on each side (3–4 minutes total) until medium rare. Remove from the pan and set aside.

2 Place the broccoli in a bowl and add a little olive oil. Season with salt and pepper and mix to coat. Grill the broccoli, turning, for 3 minutes. Break the tuna into smaller pieces, and combine with the grilled broccoli in a bowl. Add the basil and lemon juice.

3 Crush the dried chilies with the garlic and a pinch of salt to make a smooth paste. Using a fork, mix the garlic paste into the ricotta. Do not overbeat the ricotta, as you want it to still have some texture. Season well with lots of black pepper.

4 Roll the dough into a circle ¼in (½cm) thick. Spread the ricotta over the dough, leaving a ¾in (2cm) border around the edge. Scatter the tuna-broccoli mixture over half of the dough. Drizzle with a little olive oil. Fold the top edge down and, using your finger and thumb, pinch the edges together to seal. Brush the outside with a little oil, and bake in the oven for 10–12 minutes until golden brown and crisp.

This filled pizza, or calzone, came from a busy baker's shop overlooking the market in Catania. Most of the pizza emanating from this establishment never went further than about six feet outside the shopfront. The flavors of this filling were unexpected, yet spectacular—hence the 20 or so people standing and eating a slice. You could easily make this as small snack-sized calzone.

Cudduruni con patate, salsiccie e pomodori secchi Potato, spiced sausage, and sun-dried tomato pizza

Makes 6–8 small pizzas or 2 large ones

8oz (225g) new potatoes, scrubbed and
   thinly sliced

2 garlic cloves, peeled

¼ cup olive oil

1 recipe cudduruni dough (see p134)

4oz (115g) spicy Italian salami or other dried
   pork sausage such as chorizo, sliced

¼ cup chopped drained, oil-packed
   sun-dried tomatoes

4 tsp finely chopped fresh rosemary leaves

1 cup freshly grated pecorino cheese

sea salt and freshly ground black pepper

1 Preheat the oven to 425°F (220°C). Cook the potato slices in a pot of boiling water for 5 minutes, then drain in a colander and let dry. Crush the garlic with a little salt, then mix with the olive oil.

2 Once it has rested, punch down the center of the cudduruni dough to remove any air from it. Knead in the bowl for a couple of minutes. This can be made as either small individual pizzas or two larger ones. The large pizzas do not have to have an even shape; you can even make a large square slab if you wish. If making individual pizzas, break off 6–8 even-sized balls of dough, a little smaller than a tennis ball. Roll the dough out on a floured work surface until about ¼in (½cm) thick.

3 Brush the dough with the crushed garlic and olive oil mixture, then scatter the potato slices over the top. Next scatter over the sausage and sun-dried tomatoes. Sprinkle with the rosemary and finally the pecorino. Drizzle with some more of the olive oil and garlic mixture, and season well with pepper and some sea salt. (Remember that the sausage and cheese will be quite salty.)

4 Bake in the oven for 10–12 minutes or until the crust is golden brown on the bottom. Serve at once, cut into slices as needed.

This is one of two versions of pizza I ate in Sicily. It has a very tasty topping of sliced potatoes with rosemary, spiced sausage, sun-dried tomatoes, and pecorino. It is very versatile in how you can serve it—as a snack, canapé, or starter, or as an informal meal. In the bakeries of Catania, it is served in large sheets to be eaten while shopping in the market.

Imqaret Date pastries

These very popular sweet snacks are eaten hot from street stalls around the island of Malta. I first had them at the city gate in Valetta, where the vendor was in a shiny stainless-steel trailer similar to one selling hot dogs. You could see him frying large batches of the imqaret in cauldrons of boiling oil. These pastries stem from ancient recipes tracing back to Malta's Arabic past. The sweet date filling is infused with an anise flavor. These are great with coffee or tea, or with ice cream or a cream-based dessert such as crème brûlée or panna cotta.

Makes about 30

For the pastry

4 cups all-purpose flour

pinch of salt

⅓ cup sugar

4 tbsp (½ stick) unsalted butter, cut into pieces

5 tbsp dry red wine

¼ cup orange juice

For the filling

1lb (450g) pitted dates

juice and grated zest of 1 orange

juice and grated zest of 1 lemon

⅔ cup dry red wine

pinch of ground cloves

1 bay leaf

4 star anise

vegetable oil for frying

1 To make the pastry, sift the flour and salt into a large bowl. Add the sugar and butter, and rub into the flour between your fingertips to form the texture of breadcrumbs. Using a spoon, mix in the wine and orange juice to make a smooth dough, adding a little extra flour if necessary. Turn the dough out onto a floured work surface, and knead as you would bread dough, until it is soft but not sticky. Let rest in the refrigerator for at least 30 minutes until needed.

2 Combine all the ingredients for the filling in a heavy saucepan. Simmer gently over medium heat for 20 minutes until the dates are soft and the wine has reduced. Discard the star anise and the bay leaf. Transfer the filling to a food processor or blender, and process until smooth. Let cool completely.

3 Cut the pastry into 4 equal pieces. Working one piece at a time on a floured work surface, roll it out as thinly as possible, into a strip about 4in (10cm) wide. Using a pastry brush, moisten the edges with a little water, and spoon some of the filling down the center of the pastry. Fold the pastry in half lengthwise, covering the filling. Flatten slightly, and press the edges together to seal. You will end up with a long roll. Cut diagonally across the pastry with a sharp knife, making diamond-shaped pieces that are about 2in (5cm) long. Repeat with the remaining pastry and date filling.

4 In a heavy pan over medium-high heat, heat about ¾in (2cm) of oil until hot. Break off a small piece of pastry and add to the oil—it should sizzle slightly, but not brown too fast. When ready, shallow-fry the pastries in small batches for 4–5 minutes or until golden brown all over. Serve at once.

The Middle East and North Africa

The cuisine of the Middle East is as ancient and fluid as the history of its peoples. Long-established spice routes, traders, and nomadic cultures have meant similar dishes are made across a vast distance and several countries. Some food styles have not been restricted by geographical boundaries. Other dishes are particular to small regions or even groups of people, and adhere to longstanding traditions that have been handed down for generations.

Day 68: Istanbul, Turkey Istanbul, the city that straddles the continent of Europe on one side and Asia on the other, is full of contrasts and contradictions. This is apparent in the historical buildings such as the mosque of Sophia, once a spectacular Byzantine church from the third century. The layers of history and the different cultures that are present in Istanbul seem to exist in harmony. The same is true of the food. Some things are simple, such as the grilled mackerel sandwiches with tomato and onion that are available on the central bridge that crosses the Golden Horn. Other dishes are much more elaborate, with an intricate layering of exotic spices from the East. One of Istanbul's most famous examples of street food is the delicious *midye dolmasi*, a dish of plump steamed mussels stuffed with short-grain rice, raisins, pine nuts, and a heady mix of cinnamon, ground allspice, paprika, cayenne pepper, and ground cloves. Served with wedges of lemon, these mussels make a great snack. It is amazing that they can be sold so cheaply when someone has had to open the individual mussels with a knife like an oyster. It was after tasting these that I then found the grilled sardines on pp144–145.

Day 79: Marrakesh, Morocco As the February cold creeps in, dusk falls and the market in Marrakesh springs to life in the twilight. At this late hour it seems as if the entire population of Morocco is packed into the market square, which is stacked with painted stalls selling roasted pumpkin seeds, dried figs, juicy dates, apricots, and prunes. There are snake charmers and soothsayers, poets and musicians, all enthusiastically providing the mystical entertainments that have been performed for centuries. Food stalls groan under towers of pistachios and pine nuts, almonds, and walnuts. People crowd onto benches ready for their plates of hot *harira* (see pp166–167), kebabs, and spicy sausages. The hungry customers enjoy dishes of couscous with grilled lamb and other meats, including liver and brains. All are drinking fresh tamarind juice or mint tea—which is always served scalding hot and syrupy sweet. Large pots of snails are being devoured by the bowlful, and huge clouds of aromatic smoke billow from barbecues, blurring the edges of my vision. Women and men are adorned in the unique robes of their tribes, bodies wrapped in layers against the cold winter night. Jumbled into the ancient mix are poor-quality stereos blasting shallow pop music, and stalls selling mobile phone ringtones. As the scene bombards my senses, I consider my myriad choices for a hearty supper.

Samak a-sardeen mi'l'aaq

Grilled sardines

Serves 4–6

6 bay leaves, coarsely chopped

2 tbsp salt

4 green cardamom pods

2 garlic cloves

2 small dried red chilies

1 tsp ground allspice

2 tbsp olive oil

12 fresh sardines, cleaned inside and out
(you can ask your fishmonger to do this)

1 lemon, cut into quarters lengthwise, then
cut crosswise into triangular slices

½ bunch flat-leaf parsley, finely chopped

freshly ground black pepper

1 Preheat a charcoal grill, barbecue, or grill pan until white-hot. Using a pestle and mortar, grind the bay leaves with the salt until you are left with a bright green powder. (This bay leaf salt is delicious on its own and can be used to season roast potatoes or grilled meats or fish.) Add the cardamom pods and continue to grind until fine. Sift the mixture through a sieve into a bowl, and discard any husks or pieces of stalk.

2 Crush the garlic, dried chilies, and allspice, again using a pestle and mortar, and mix with the other spices in a bowl. Add the olive oil.

3 Pat the inside of the sardines dry with paper towels, then rub some of the spice marinade over the inside and outside of each fish. Mix the lemon slices with the remaining spice marinade. Season with lots of pepper. Mix in the parsley. Stuff the sardines with the lemon and parsley mixture.

4 Grill the sardines for 3–4 minutes on each side or until golden brown and crispy on both sides. With small fish such as this, it is important not to overcook the fish—otherwise it will dry out. As the sardines are small and the grill or pan is hot, remember that the sardines will continue cooking when removed from the heat.

5 Serve these fantastic little fish hot with wedges of lemon, a selection of salads, and lots of fresh bread. The salt, sourness, and heat of the spice marinade and the lemon slices cut the richness of the fish.

I had these spicy fresh sardines in a small café overlooking the majestic stretch of water in Istanbul called the Golden Horn. I settled back to enjoy my sardines and the view of Istanbul's skyline, liberally scattered with its magnificent mosques, minarets, and other historical architectural wonders. This dish is a classic example of street food that has a simplicity belying its tastiness, relying as it does on the best and freshest ingredients. It is great for a barbecue. The stuffing can also be used for mackerel, red mullet, sea bass, bream (porgy), or snapper.

Fetta Stuffed eggplant with yogurt and pine nuts

Fetta is traditionally eaten for breakfast in Lebanon and Syria, and is a very substantial start to the day. I had this version in a small café in Beirut, for an early breakfast before being taken to other similar streetside cafés and breakfast establishments to sample other dishes commonly eaten at the start of a working day. On that particular day, I ate eight different breakfasts across the city, each one as individually filling as this fetta with its irresistible finishing touch of hot garlic-spiked yogurt.

Serves 4–6

2 eggplants, about 2¼lb (1kg) in total

olive oil for frying

7 pita breads, broken into small triangles, plus extra for serving

¾ cup pine nuts

1¼lb (550g) minced or ground lamb

1 tsp ground allspice, plus a little extra

1 cup tomato juice

1 cinnamon stick

2 bay leaves

2 garlic cloves

1 cup Greek-style yogurt

salt and freshly ground black pepper

1 Cut the tops off the eggplants and scoop out half of the flesh. Soak the eggplants in salted water while you prepare the other ingredients.

2 Heat some olive oil in a heavy pan over medium-high heat. Cook the triangles of pita bread in batches, turning, until crisp and golden brown. Remove from the oil using tongs, and drain on paper towels. Using the same pan, cook the pine nuts in the oil until golden brown. Remove and drain on paper towels.

3 Add a little oil to another frying pan. Cook the meat with the 1 tsp allspice until the meat is cooked throughout. Season with salt and pepper, and stir in half the pine nuts. Remove the eggplant shells from the water and drain well. Stuff the scooped-out cavities with the meat mixture. Cook the stuffed eggplants in the oil, filling-side up, until lightly browned on the bottom, being careful not to disturb the filling.

4 Heat the tomato juice with the cinnamon stick and bay leaves in a large shallow pan. Season with salt and pepper. When the tomato juice is simmering, add the stuffed eggplants and cook gently until the sauce thickens. Meanwhile, heat a broiler until hot.

5 Crush the garlic and add to the yogurt. Cover the bottom of an ovenproof dish with fried pita bread, then arrange the stuffed eggplants and pour the yogurt over the top. Drizzle with the tomato sauce and then the yogurt mixture. Sprinkle with a little extra allspice. Place the dish under the broiler. Cook for a few minutes until heated through and the yogurt is hot and sizzling in places. Garnish with the remaining toasted pine nuts, and serve hot with lots of warm pita bread.

Kibbeh samak Stuffed fish balls

Serves 4–6

1lb (450g) bulghur (cracked wheat)

1 onion, finely chopped

1½lb (700g) boneless firm white fish

juice of ½ lemon

vegetable oil for frying

salt and freshly ground black pepper

lemon wedges for serving

fresh cilantro for garnish

For the filling

1 tbsp olive oil

1 onion, finely chopped

⅓ cup dried apricots (about 7), finely
   chopped

¼ cup pitted dates (about 4), finely chopped

small handful of chopped cilantro leaves

1 In a large bowl, cover the bulghur wheat with cold water, and let soak for 10 minutes. Put the onion into a food processor and process until smooth. Add the fish and lemon juice, and season with salt and pepper.

2 Line a sieve with a clean fine dish towel or a piece of cheesecloth, and drain the soaked bulghur. Pick up the ends of the cloth and squeeze tightly to remove any excess liquid. Working in batches, add the bulghur to the fish purée, processing between each addition to form a workable dough. If it needs to be a bit more malleable, add a little ice water.

3 To make the filling, heat the oil in a heavy pan over medium-high heat. Sauté the onion for 3–4 minutes until softened. Add the apricots, dates, and cilantro. Season with salt and pepper. Remove from the heat and let cool.

4 With moistened hands, divide the fish mixture into 20 or so pieces, and roll into even-sized balls. Using your index finger, make a hole in each ball and fill it with a little of the fruit stuffing. Re-form the ball around the stuffing to enclose completely, and pat into shape. Heat the oil for deep-frying. Cook the fish balls in batches until they are golden brown on all sides. Drain on paper towels.

5 Garnish with fresh cilantro, and serve warm with lemon wedges. You can easily vary the filling given here slightly, using some chopped nuts, spices, or chopped fresh chilies, or more chopped herbs to suit your taste. Serve as an appetizer or as part of a larger selection of dishes, or as a snack or canapé.

In the ancient Lebanese coastal ports of Sidon and Tyre, cities that were strategically important before the arrival of the Romans, fried patties or cakes known as "kibbeh" are made from fish and stuffed with dried fruits. Kibbeh are usually made with lamb and are a traditional snack across Lebanon and the Middle East. Varieties range from spicy to mild; with nuts or without. Some use prime minced lamb and are eaten raw; others are fried or baked. Their shape varies from small balls to large egg shapes or flatter pockets, like small pita breads.

Shourba corbasi
Chard soup with rice and turmeric

Serves 4–6

1lb (450g) chard or spinach leaves, or beet
    leaves (stalks removed), or a combination
    of all three
1 quart good-quality vegetable or
    chicken stock
2 tbsp olive oil
2 onions, finely chopped
2 leeks, trimmed and rinsed, halved
    lengthwise, and thinly sliced

½ cup long-grain white rice
2 tbsp white wine vinegar
2 garlic cloves, finely chopped
1½ cups plain Greek-style yogurt
large pinch of ground turmeric
juice of 1 lemon
½ bunch of fresh mint leaves, coarsely
    chopped
salt and freshly ground black pepper

This wholesome springtime soup is commonly served all over the Mediterranean and Middle East. It uses the freshest ingredients and, as the vegetables are not cooked for long, the soup keeps its bright color, all its flavor, and therefore its nutrients. Try different combinations of greens—spinach and beet leaves also work well. I had this soup at a simple café within a vegetable market where all these vegetables were being sold. In terms of distance, the food traveled a matter of a few feet from market stall to saucepan. Serve in spring and early summer.

1 Finely dice the stalks of the chard leaves. Rinse the leaves and finely shred. Bring the stock to a boil in a saucepan.

2 Heat the oil in a heavy pan or casserole over medium-high heat. Add the onion, leek, and chard stems, and cook over low heat for 4–5 minutes until slightly colored. Add the rice and cook, stirring occasionally for 2 minutes, to coat. Season with salt and pepper. Pour in the hot stock and vinegar, and bring to a boil. Once boiling, reduce the heat and simmer for 12–15 minutes or until the rice is tender. While the soup is simmering, mince the garlic with a little salt. Stir into the yogurt with the turmeric and half the lemon juice. Mix together, then taste and season with salt and pepper.

3 When the rice is tender, add the shredded chard leaves to the soup. Simmer for about 3 minutes until the leaves are tender. Remove from the heat and whisk in the yogurt mixture, then add the mint. Check the seasoning, adding a little extra lemon juice or cracked black pepper if needed. Serve warm or at room temperature, to best appreciate the flavors.

Beet tops Beet leaves, or tops, make a great extra vegetable, which you often get for free when you buy beets. They are delicious when blanched and sautéed, providing a delicious sweetness combined with an irony earthiness. The Italians use beet tops a lot; they make a wonderful addition to a ravioli filling.

Kofte samak Harissa mini fish cakes with preserved lemon

Serves 4–6

1 tbsp olive oil

1 garlic clove, finely chopped

1 tbsp coriander seeds, crushed

1 tsp paprika

1lb (450g) firm white fish fillets (such as
   hake, snapper, sea bream (porgy), or
   cod), skin and bones removed

rind of ½ preserved lemon, any white pith
   removed and rind finely diced (see below)

4 scallions (green onions), thinly sliced

½ bunch of fresh cilantro, coarsely chopped

2 tsp harissa sauce (available in cans or jars
   in Middle Eastern markets)

1 egg

juice of ½ lemon

vegetable oil for frying

salt and freshly ground black pepper

These small fish cakes are full of flavors from Morocco and the North African coast. Harissa is a hot, fiery spice paste used across the Middle East. Preserved lemon is another ingredient that crops up in Moroccan cuisine, and it is easy to make yourself. An added bonus is that storing it under oil infuses that oil with a lemon flavor.

1 In a small pan, heat the olive oil and cook the garlic and coriander seeds until golden brown and fragrant. Stir in the paprika and remove from the heat.

2 Put the fish in a food processor with the aromatic cooked spice mixture, the preserved lemon rind, scallions, and cilantro. Add in the harissa and egg, and season with salt and pepper. Add half of the lemon juice and process until smooth.

3 Heat the vegetable oil in large frying pan over medium-high heat. Cook a small piece of the mixture and taste to check the seasoning. Adjust with salt and pepper, and an extra squeeze of fresh lemon juice if needed. Roll the fish cakes into 16 equal portions. Cook in small batches until golden brown on all sides. Drain on paper towels.

4 Serve with a cucumber salad dressed with ground cinnamon and a little orange juice, or as a canapé with drinks before a meal.

Preserved lemons Place 2 lemons in a small saucepan with a tight-fitting lid. Cover with cold water. Add 3 heaping tablespoons sea salt (the salt removes the bitterness from the skin). Bring the water to a boil, and simmer for 10–12 minutes or until the lemons are soft when pierced with the tip of a knife. Remove with a slotted spoon and refresh under cold running water. When cool, cut in half. Using a sharp knife, remove all the flesh and white pith. Trim down the lemon skin from the inside, so only the lemon zest remains. Cover the lemon zest with olive oil and you have preserved lemon; it keeps covered in the refrigerator for up to 6 weeks.

Bolani Afghani flat bread

Makes 6–8

4 cups all-purpose flour

1 tsp salt

3 eggs, lightly beaten

⅔ cup olive oil plus extra for cooking

1 Sift the flour and salt into a bowl. Make a well in the center, and add the eggs, olive oil, and 1 cup water. Bring together to make a ball of dough. Knead on a floured work surface for 10–15 minutes until very soft and elastic. Roll the dough into balls each roughly the size of a tennis ball. Cover with a damp cloth, and let rest for 30 minutes.

2 Oil the work surface and spread out one of the balls of dough, gently pulling the edges to stretch it as thin and wide as possible, as if you are making a strudel. Dust the surface with a little flour, and fold the pastry over and over to make a pleated fan. Roll up this pleated piece of dough to make a curled ball. Repeat with the remaining balls of dough. Let rest, covered with a damp cloth, for another 15 minutes.

3 Heat a heavy frying pan over medium-high heat. Use your hands to pat a curled ball of dough into a circle about 8in (20cm) in diameter. Add a little oil to the pan, and cook the flat disc of dough, turning once, so it is golden brown on each side. Repeat with the remaining balls of dough. Serve warm, accompanied by Roast Pumpkin Paste (p154) and Carrot Pickle (p155).

Bolani is a delicious flaky flat bread. I spent a very enjoyable afternoon with a man called Billal in the Oakland Farmers' Market near San Francisco. His East West Gourmet company makes breads, relishes, and dips from his native Afghanistan. The recipes here and on pp154–155 are authentic street food specials available at small stalls, cafés, and markets for generations. Every time I make this flat bread I think of Billal's generosity. When I asked for his card he just gave me another bag of flat bread, saying cheerily that it had his number on the front.

Kadu Roast pumpkin paste

Serves 6–8

1 sweet, firm-fleshed pumpkin or butternut
 squash, about 2¼lb (1kg)

2 garlic cloves, finely chopped

1 tbsp ground coriander

2 tbsp olive oil

juice of ½ lemon

salt and freshly ground black pepper

This is one of the many dips I tasted at Billal's stall during my visit there (see p153). Roasting the pumpkin whole means that the roasted skin imparts its delicious nutty smoked flavor to the inside flesh. It is similar to roasting eggplant for baba ghanoush. Indeed, all the dips and relishes I tasted at Billal's stall were delicious, with a striking contrast between sweet and hot ingredients. There was a curried eggplant and tomato paste, and one made with spiced spinach. The spicy Carrot Pickle (opposite) worked best with the sweet pumpkin.

1 Roast the pumpkin whole on a baking sheet in a preheated 400°F (200°C) oven until soft and caramelized, about 40 minutes to an hour, depending on the size. Do not make any cuts or incisions in the flesh because you will lose juice and flavor. Let the pumpkin cool, then cut in half. Scoop out the seeds and discard, then remove the soft cooked flesh and mash. Cut up about one-third of the cooked pumpkin skin. Chop finely, and mix with the pumpkin flesh.

2 Mix the garlic with the ground coriander. Heat a heavy frying pan and add the olive oil. Cook the garlic and coriander until fragrant. Add the cooked pumpkin mixture and season well with salt and pepper. Add the lemon juice and taste. Adjust the seasoning as necessary. The flavors will be sweet and nutty, with a background of heat from the pepper, garlic, and coriander. The lemon juice provides the mixture with an edge and definition. The pumpkin flesh will be sweet and bland, and can take a lot of seasoning.

Turshi zardak Carrot pickle

Makes 4 large jars

1 tbsp olive oil	2 tsp ground coriander
6 garlic cloves, finely chopped	1 tsp ground allspice
3 fresh red jalapeño or serrano chilies, seeded and finely chopped	6½lb (3kg) carrots, peeled and finely grated
1 tsp cayenne pepper	2½ cups sugar
2 tsp ground cumin	2 cups malt vinegar
	salt and freshly ground black pepper

1 Heat the oil in a heavy Dutch oven or other large saucepan over medium-high heat for 2–3 minutes. Add the garlic and chilies, and cook for a couple of minutes until fragrant. Sprinkle in the cayenne pepper, cumin, coriander, and allspice. Cook for another minute or two. Add the carrot, sugar, and vinegar, and simmer gently over low heat for 40 minutes to 1 hour, or until the excess liquid has evaporated and the mixture is thick and syrupy. Season with salt and pepper. The pickle should be hot and spicy, but sweet with a pronounced sourness.

2 Spoon the pickle into sterilized glass jars with tight-fitting lids. Seal while the pickle is still hot, to create a vacuum. Let sit at least 24 hours for the flavors to blend before using. Store in a cool, dark place.

To enjoy a fantastic combination of flavors, take one of the hot bolani on p153 and spread with the roast pumpkin paste (opposite). Add some hummus or a little yogurt. Spoon on the Carrot Pickle, then scatter with some fresh cilantro leaves, roll it all up, and be prepared for a flavor sensation. The combination of everything in one mouthful makes for a fantastic set of tastes. You could use pita or naan bread to get great results as a snack. Treat this pickle like any chutney or relish. It can be put with cold meats or cheese, and complements just about anything it is paired with.

Fattoush Toasted pita bread salad

Fattoush is a marvelous combination of simple flavors and textures that creates a result that is much more than the sum of its parts. Eaten at any time of day, it is often enjoyed as part of a mezze or accompanying grilled meat, kebabs, or chicken, or some fried falafel. It is a great way of using up stale pita bread. The drier the bread, the more juice it absorbs. In Lebanese cooking lots of fresh herbs are used; this salad is no exception. Fresh and healthy, fattoush packs a tight punch for the taste buds. As a result it assumes near cult status with anyone who tries it.

Serves 4–6

2 large pita bread, broken into pieces and toasted lightly
juice of about 1½ lemons
2 garlic cloves
4 ripe plum tomatoes, halved, seeded, and cut into ½in (1cm) dice
1 cucumber, halved, seeded, and cut into ½in (1cm) dice

1 tbsp ground sumac (available in Middle Eastern markets)
4 scallions (green onions), thinly sliced
handful of fresh arugula leaves
½ bunch of flat-leaf parsley leaves
½ bunch of mint leaves
½ cup extra virgin olive oil
salt and freshly ground black pepper

1 Place the toasted bread pieces in a large bowl. Add the juice of ½ lemon, and season well with salt and pepper.

2 Crush the garlic cloves with a little salt until you have a smooth purée. In a small bowl, combine the tomato and cucumber with the garlic purée. Season with salt and pepper, the sumac, and some more lemon juice. Add to the toasted bread, along with the scallions, arugula, parsley, and mint. Drizzle in the olive oil and toss gently to mix.

3 Taste the salad, adding more lemon if needed. It should be sour from the lemon juice and peppery hot from the arugula and seasoning. The tomatoes and cucumber will be sweet, and the sumac is a grand spice that is purple in color and provides an essential lemony, peppery element to the flavor of the salad. Serve at once, as the lemon juice will begin to discolor the greens.

Salatet kousa Zucchini salad

Serves 4–6

2¼lb (1kg) small zucchini, ends trimmed
   (they should be not much longer than a
   man's index finger)

¼ cup extra virgin olive oil

1 garlic clove, crushed

2 tsp paprika

½ tsp ground cumin

½ tsp chili powder

3 tbsp lemon juice

30 flat-leaf parsley leaves, coarsely chopped

salt and freshly ground black pepper

This is a fresh and simple mezze-style dish which could accompany other vegetable dishes or meat or fish. When putting different dishes together, think about the dominant flavors present in each one, to avoid repetition. Colors and textures are also very important. Some dishes can be crisp and spicy; others could be a paste or a dip such as hummus or baba ghanoush. One could contain tahini; another could have roast almonds or pine nuts. Put them all together, and you have a colorful selection of dishes with variety in looks, ingredients, and tastes.

1 Cut the zucchini into quarters lengthwise. (Do not use zucchini that are too thick because the inside will not be firm, but rather full of watery seeds. If small zucchini are not available, cut the outside flesh away from the central core of the zucchini and discard the central core of seeds.)

2 Heat a heavy frying pan over medium-high heat. Add a little oil and cook the zucchini in batches until golden brown on both sides. (Cooking in batches helps to ensure that the temperature of the pan does not drop, which would result in the vegetables steaming or boiling in their own juices. Also, do not overcook, otherwise the zucchini will be soggy.)

3 Meanwhile, crush the garlic with a little salt and combine with the spices, the remaining olive oil, and the lemon juice. Place the cooked zucchini in a bowl, and cover with the dressing. Let sit for 1 hour to blend flavors before serving. Taste and adjust the seasoning as needed, then garnish with the parsley. Serve with grilled meat or fish, or as part of a selection of mezze to start the meal.

Salatet semsum Sesame salad

Serves 6 as part of a mezze

1 garlic clove	30 flat-leaf parsley leaves, chopped
large pinch of sea salt	½ tsp coarse-ground black pepper
½ cup tahini (sesame seed paste)	3 tbsp extra virgin olive oil
1 tbsp white vinegar	juice of ½ lemon
3 cucumbers, cut into small cubes	2 tbsp sesame seeds, toasted
4 scallions (green onions), thinly sliced	

1 Crush the garlic with the salt until smooth. Add the tahini, and stir in the white vinegar until the mixture reaches the consistency of yogurt. Stir in the cucumber, scallions, parsley, and pepper. Add the remaining olive oil and the lemon juice, tossing gently to mix.

2 Serve alongside kofte kebab (see pp176–177) or grilled chicken, garnished with the toasted sesame seeds.

Mezze is a great way to start a meal, and there are hundreds of variations of little dishes that can be served with olives, pickles, and lots of hot bread. Tahini is a very important ingredient in the Middle East. This paste made from sesame seeds is present in hummus and a sauce called tarator (see p185). Mezze is often eaten at a small café or stall with friends, before going to eat at home with family. The idea behind this style of eating is that it is a collection of flavors and textures in different dishes. Eaten together, they complement and contrast one another.

Dzhazh garfa pilaf bil iluz Eastern jeweled pilaf with cinnamon and almonds

This juicy and aromatic chicken dish is bejeweled with shining fried raisins, chopped dates, almonds, and onions flecked with strands of saffron. The succulent dried fruits and colorful, fragrant spices create an image of the exotic East, a land of jewels, silks, and mystique. I enjoyed many variations of this in Jordan and Turkey. It can be eaten hot or cold, and is visually striking because of the caramelized onions and bright orange turmeric and saffron. It could be made using baby chickens, partridge, or quail, allowing one small bird per person.

Serves 8

¼ cup olive oil	½ tsp ground turmeric
3 cinnamon sticks	½ tsp ground cinnamon
6 green cardamom pods	¼ tsp ground cardamom
10 black peppercorns	1½ tbsp butter
3 onions, finely chopped	½ cup almonds
1 cup tomato juice	½ cup raisins
2 medium chickens, each disjointed into at least 4 pieces	¼ cup chopped dates
	½ tsp saffron threads, crushed
3 cups long-grain white rice, rinsed	salt and freshly ground black pepper

1 Preheat the broiler until medium-hot. Heat a heavy pan over medium-high heat and add 1 tbsp of the olive oil. Add the whole spices—cinnamon sticks, cardamom pods, and peppercorns—and cook for a couple of minutes, stirring, until fragrant. Add about one-third of the onion and cook until soft and barely golden. Add the tomato juice and 3½ cups water, season with salt, and bring to a boil. Reduce the heat to a gentle simmer and add the chicken pieces; cook gently for about 10 minutes. Remove the chicken from the broth, sprinkle the chicken with half the ground spices, and set aside.

2 Pour the rice into the broth. Cook over high heat until the liquid is almost absorbed, then reduce heat to low and continue cooking until tender. Remove from the heat and let sit, covered, until needed.

3 Place the chicken on a baking sheet, and cook, turning once, under the broiler until golden brown all over. In a separate frying pan, melt half the butter and fry the almonds until golden brown. Transfer to a small bowl. Cook the raisins and dates in the same pan. When soft, add to the almonds. Melt the remaining butter, and cook the remaining onion until golden brown. Add the rest of the ground spices and the saffron to the onion. Season with salt and pepper.

4 To serve, stir the onion mixture into the rice with half the almond and fruit mixture. Place the rice in a dish with the chicken pieces on top. Scatter the remaining almond and fruit mixture over the top.

Kebab b'il karaz

Lamb meatballs with sour cherry sauce

Serves 6–8

¾ cup pitted dried sour (tart) cherries

1 tbsp sugar

1 tbsp pomegranate molasses

juice of 1 lemon

For the meatballs

2 garlic cloves, halved and any green inner
  shoots removed

2 small dried red chilies, finely chopped

2 tsp ground coriander

pinch of salt

a little olive oil

1 onion, finely chopped

1lb (450g) ground lamb

½ bunch flat-leaf parsley, coarsely chopped

freshly ground black pepper

1 Put the dried cherries in a heavy pan. Add 1 cup water and the sugar and pomegranate molasses. Bring to a boil, then reduce the heat and simmer gently for 30 minutes until the sauce is thick and syrupy. When reduced, add the lemon juice and taste, adjusting the seasoning if necessary (bearing in mind that the meatballs will be salty, rich, and peppery-hot).

2 Meanwhile, make the meatballs. Crush the garlic, dried chilies, and ground coriander with a pinch of salt to make a paste. Heat a heavy frying pan over medium-high heat and add a little olive oil. Cook the paste for about 2 minutes until fragrant. Add the onion and sauté quickly, stirring, for 4 minutes. Remove from the heat, and transfer the onion mixture to a bowl with the lamb. Add the parsley and season well with salt and pepper. Roll the meat into small balls about the size of cherry tomatoes.

3 Heat a clean heavy pan over medium-high heat. Add a little olive oil, and cook the meatballs in small batches until golden brown all over. Drain on paper towels. Add the meatballs to the cherry sauce. Cook for a couple of minutes to blend the flavors. Serve as part of a large meal, as one of many dishes of simple grilled and marinated meats, vegetables, with lots of bread.

Sour cherries The fresh sour cherries that are traditionally used for this dish are of such good quality that they are a bit difficult to come by unless you have a good Persian, Iranian, Turkish, or Lebanese grocer nearby. Dried sour cherries make a perfect substitute and are available from supermarkets.

This dish is an unusually striking combination of flavors that makes your taste buds tingle. It works well with something quite neutral in taste because it is very rich. It hails from an area of Turkey in the south, near the Aleppo region in Syria. I have had variations of this in both Turkey and Syria. When I first had these meatballs, they came at the end of a vast meal, yet room was made on the table and in our stomachs. The sizzling serving dish was scraped clean, and the extra sauce mopped up with copious amounts of flat bread.

Fatayer bisabanikh Spinach pastries

These triangular pastries
have remained unchanged
for centuries. Variations
of this would have been
made in the Levant region
at the time of the crusades.
In the days when everyone
baked their own bread,
the home cook would make
enough dough for the whole
week's worth of bread and
these savory pastries.
Fillings vary hugely from
spinach or chard, to
mushroom, cheese, or lamb,
and can be spiked with
spices or be quite plain.
The same dough is used
for small crescent-shaped
pastries, called "samboosak,"
which are often fried; the
triangular ones are baked.

Makes 25–30 pastries

For the pastry

2 envelopes (¼oz each) active dry yeast

3½ cups all-purpose flour

1 tsp salt

2 tbsp olive oil

For the filling

2lb (900g) spinach, stems discarded,
  rinsed, and drained in a colander

1 pomegranate

3 tbsp olive oil

1 onion, finely grated or very finely chopped

2 garlic cloves, finely chopped

¾ cup pine nuts

¾ cup walnuts

1 tsp ground sumac (optional)

juice of 1½ lemons

salt and freshly ground black pepper

1 To make the pastry, mix the yeast in a small bowl with a spoonful of the flour and a small amount of water to make a paste. Stir in ½ cup lukewarm water, and let sit in a warm place for 10 minutes. Sift the flour and salt into a large bowl. Make a well in the center, add the oil and the yeast mixture, and mix together. Gradually add another ½ cup lukewarm water until incorporated. Turn the dough onto a floured surface. Knead for 15 minutes until shiny and elastic. Form into a ball, and place in a lightly oiled large bowl. Cover with plastic wrap or a clean towel. Let rise in a warm place for about 2 hours until it doubles in volume.

2 Chop the spinach leaves and squeeze dry. Remove the seeds from the pomegranate (see tip on p36), and put in a bowl with the juice. Heat the oil in a heavy pan over medium-low heat. Add the onion and cook for 3–5 minutes until soft. Push to one side of the pan. Add the garlic, pine nuts, and walnuts. Increase the heat to medium and cook the garlic and nuts until golden brown. Mix the nuts into the onion mixture, and reduce the heat. Add the spinach and cook for 2–3 minutes until wilted. Add the sumac (if using), pomegranate seeds, and lemon juice. Check the seasoning. Remove from the heat and set aside.

3 Preheat the oven to 375°F (190°C). Break off the pieces of dough and form into 25–30 equal-sized balls. Roll into thin discs on a floured work surface. Put a teaspoon of filling in the center of each disc (don't include too much liquid). Bring up the sides of the dough to form a three-sided packet, pinch the edges together firmly, and place on an oiled baking sheet. Bake in the oven for 5 minutes, then reduce the temperature to 350°F (180°C). Bake for 15 minutes longer.

Harira Spicy bean soup

Serves 6

½ cup dried chickpeas (garbanzo beans)

½ cup dried cannellini beans or fava beans
  or butter beans

½ cup dried split green peas

1 tsp baking soda

1 tbsp coriander seeds

1 tbsp cumin seeds

2 small dried chilies

1 tsp ground cloves

½ tsp cayenne pepper

2in (5cm) piece of fresh ginger, peeled
  and grated

3 garlic cloves

  olive oil for cooking

1 cinnamon stick

3 onions, finely chopped

8 ripe tomatoes, coarsely grated (see tip
  in method on p173)

½ cup red or yellow lentils, picked and rinsed

juice of 1 lemon plus a little extra to finish

½ bunch of fresh cilantro, leaves coarsely
  chopped

salt and freshly ground black pepper

During the Muslim fast of Ramadan you are allowed to eat only after the sun has gone down, and you also eat little or no meat. As a result there are lots of substantial vegetarian dishes, such as this bean soup, that are sold at the food stalls and in the night markets after the sun has set. You can use any combination of dried beans, lentils, or chickpeas for this hearty soup, as well as different blends of spices. The flavors improve over 24 hours, blending and softening. Serve with a spoon of cooling yogurt in the center of each bowl and lots of fresh crusty bread.

1 Soak the chickpeas and cannellini beans overnight in plenty of cold water. The split green peas need only be soaked for 2 hours. Drain and rinse the chickpeas and beans. Put in a large pan, cover with lots of cold water, and add the baking soda. Bring to a boil over medium heat. Reduce the heat, and simmer for 40–60 minutes until the beans are cooked, but not mushy. As they are simmering, skim off any scum that rises to the top. Drain and rinse.

2 Meanwhile, using a pestle and mortar, grind the coriander seeds, cumin seeds, and dried chilies into a fine powder. Add the cloves, cayenne pepper, ginger, and garlic, and work into a paste. Heat 2 tbsp oil in a heavy pan over medium-high heat. Add the spice mixture and cinnamon stick. Cook for 2 minutes, stirring frequently, until fragrant. Reduce the heat to medium, add the onion, and cook for about 10 minutes until the onion starts to brown. Add the tomato pulp; cook until any excess liquid has evaporated. Rinse the split green peas, mix into the tomato mixture with the lentils. Next add 7 cups water. Bring to a boil, reduce the heat, and simmer for 20 minutes. Add the rinsed chickpeas and beans. Mix together. Season well and add the lemon juice. Add half the cilantro. Let the soup sit off the heat for 5 minutes, then check the seasoning.

3 To serve, garnish with the remaining cilantro and a little extra squeeze of lemon juice. This soup can be eaten hot or warm at any time of the year.

Baba ghanoush
Smoky roast eggplant dip

Serves 4–6

3 eggplants	juice of ½ lemon
2 garlic cloves, finely chopped	½ cup extra virgin olive oil
pinch of salt	2 tbsp crème fraîche
1 tbsp tahini (sesame seed paste)	or Greek-style yogurt
½ tsp cayenne pepper	freshly ground black pepper

This classic Lebanese eggplant dip is the perfect accompaniment to cheese, salad, or grilled meat. It works particularly well with the smoky rich flavors of rare grilled beef or lamb. I have made this recipe slightly smoother and richer by adding crème fraîche; yogurt could be added instead. Throughout my travels in the Middle East I had never tired of this delicious dip, eaten with lots of freshly baked bread. Once you make some yourself, you will never again be satisfied with the store-bought version.

1 Place the eggplants either directly on a preheated grill or under a very hot broiler. Roast the eggplants for 10–12 minutes until the skin is blistered and charred on all sides. Keep turning the eggplants with tongs while they are cooking. Remove from the heat and place in a bowl. Cover with plastic wrap and let cool. (As the eggplants cool, steam is trapped, which in turn continues to cook the eggplants and helps loosen the charred skin.) When the eggplants are cool, remove from the bowl and pull away and discard the blackened skin. Cut the peeled eggplants into chunks.

2 Crush the garlic with a pinch of salt. Put the garlic and eggplant flesh into the food processor. Add the tahini and season with the cayenne, salt, and pepper. Process until smooth, then add the lemon juice. With the motor running, gradually add the olive oil in a thin, steady stream to make a paste (similar to making mayonnaise). When it is all combined, stir in the crème fraîche.

3 Check the seasoning. There should be a smoky sweetness from the roasted eggplant, while the tahini and salt provide a savory component. The lemon juice and crème fraîche are sour, and the black pepper is hot and peppery. Adjust the seasoning as necessary. Serve in a bowl as an accompaniment to other dishes, or as a dip with lots of fresh bread.

Labneh Yogurt cream cheese dip

Serves 8 as a dip or part of a mezze

3½ cups sheep's or goat's milk yogurt

1 tsp salt

1 tbsp olive oil

paprika or ground cumin, to garnish

1 Place the yogurt in a bowl with the salt. Whisk together to blend. Place a colander in the sink, and line with a clean fine-weave wet cloth such as muslin or cheesecloth, or even a finely woven dishcloth. Pour in the yogurt, and tie the corners of the cloth around the faucet. Let the liquid drain from the cloth for about 12 hours or overnight.

2 To serve, transfer the drained yogurt to a serving bowl. Mix the olive oil, and scatter a little paprika or cumin over the top as a garnish. Enjoy as a dip with lots of fresh bread or as one of a number of dishes served mezze-style. Don't be deceived by the simple recipe and method; the flavor of the yogurt is completely transformed.

Labneh is an essential taste of the Middle East. It is eaten in many guises at all times of the day, as a snack or part of a whole meal. Although labneh is traditionally made from goat's milk yogurt, Greek sheep's milk yogurt is a great substitute. It is very popular as a mezze-style dip eaten with kofte kebabs (see pp176–177) or falafel. It is delicious plain or can be flavored with crushed garlic, chopped chilies, ground cumin, or paprika, or some freshly chopped mint. It can be made into a more substantial dip by adding chopped cucumber, or scallion and tomato.

Shlada al falfla hamra al khizzou

Carrot and orange salad with
paprika dressing

This is a deliciously simple and effective salad that I had at a small stall in Marrakesh. Some grilled chicken marinated with harissa accompanied it. This salad has got so much going on in the dressing, and yet all your taste buds are stimulated in unison. There are also lots of different textures. The juicy oranges contrast with the crisp carrot and crunchy sesame seeds. Serve with simple grilled and roasted meats, or with something more complex. It can be a small part of a larger collection of dishes, and makes a good addition to a barbecue or picnic.

Serves 4–6

3 tbsp sesame seeds

3 or 4 generous handfuls of arugula or
  lettuce leaves

1lb (450g) carrots, peeled and grated

2 oranges, peeled, bitter white pith
  removed, and flesh cut into segments

juice of 1 lemon

30 fresh flat-leaf parsley leaves,
  coarsely chopped

salt and freshly ground black pepper

Paprika dressing

1 tsp honey

¼ tsp salt

1 tbsp water

½ tsp paprika

1 tsp mustard

¼ cup extra virgin olive oil

1 tbsp red wine vinegar

freshly ground black pepper

1 Roast the sesame seeds in a dry frying pan over medium-high heat for a few minutes; take care they do not burn. Remove from the heat.

2 Arrange the arugula in a bowl with the carrot and orange segments. Season with salt and pepper. Squeeze the lemon juice over the top, and sprinkle with the flat-leaf parsley.

3 Place all the ingredients for the dressing in a glass jar with a tight-fitting lid, add 1 tbsp water, and shake to blend thoroughly. Pour over the salad, and garnish with the toasted sesame seeds.

Lahem bil ajine Lebanese lamb pizza

Makes 15–20

1 recipe of yeast dough (see p164),
   kneaded until elastic and shiny

2 tbsp olive oil

4 onions, finely chopped

8 large plum tomatoes

1lb (450g) ground lamb

2 tsp ground coriander

1 tsp Lebanese spice mix (see p218)

1 tbsp tomato purée

1 tbsp pomegranate molasses

1 tsp brown sugar

3½oz (100g) pine nuts

small handful of fresh cilantro,
   coarsely chopped

small handful of fresh flat-leaf parsley,
   coarsely chopped

salt and freshly ground black pepper

Greek-style yogurt or tahini, for serving

lemon wedges, for serving

These are a delicious floppy sort of pizza or open-faced pie. Lamb is traditionally used, but you could also use beef. You could also make a vegetarian version with lots of sautéed mushrooms. Much smaller in size than an Italian pizza, you would generally buy a few of these to be eaten on the go. They are baked in wood ovens in bakeries and roadside cafés from Istanbul to Beirut and Damascus, and everywhere in between. Some versions are spicy, while others are a little more subtle. The pomegranate molasses used here adds great depth of flavor to the meat.

1. Prepare the dough following the instructions on p164. To make the topping, heat the oil in a large heavy frying pan, sauté pan, or Dutch oven, over medium-high heat. Add the onions and cook for 4 minutes until soft but not too brown.

2. Meanwhile, cut the tomatoes in half. Hold one of the halves with the skin side in the palm of your hand. Using a large grater, grate the flesh of the tomato. (This is a great way of making tomato pulp without having to blanch and peel the tomatoes; the skin remains in your hand and can be discarded.) Set aside.

3. Add the lamb to the onion mixture, and cook for 4–5 minutes until browned, breaking up any large pieces of meat with a spatula. Season with the spices and a good amount of salt and pepper. Add the grated tomato pulp, tomato purée, pomegranate molasses, and sugar. Cook for another 5 minutes or until any liquid has evaporated. Stir in the pine nuts, cilantro, and flat-leaf parsley. Taste and adjust the seasoning as needed. Remove from the heat, and let the mixture cool.

4. Meanwhile, preheat the oven to 425°F (220°C). Break the dough off into 15–20 equal-sized balls. Roll each ball into rounds or oval shapes on a floured work surface. Lightly spread the meat and pine nut filling onto the rolled pastry, leaving a border around the edge. Place the pizzas on one or more oiled baking sheets, and bake for 12–15 minutes or until the pastry is crisp and golden. Serve at once, with a little yogurt or tahini spooned over the top, or simply served with a wedge of lemon.

Qesbur sharmula hut
Coriander marinated fish

From Turkey to Morocco, the people of the countries bordering the Eastern and Southern Mediterranean eat a great deal of fish, often cooked whole. Freshly cooked fish is a very popular dish at street stalls and markets. Often the ovens, grills, and hot charcoal are only yards from the fish markets, or the water's edge itself. This simple recipe can be used for any whole fish, whatever the size. It works just as well with a sea bass or snapper, fresh-caught mackerel or plump sardines, or even fish steaks. It can be served as the centerpiece of a large summer barbecue or buffet.

Serves 4–6

1 large white firm-fleshed fish such as bass, snapper, or sea bream (porgy), about 4½lb (2kg)

3 garlic cloves, finely chopped

1 tsp ground coriander

1 tsp ground cumin

3 tbsp olive oil

½ cup finely chopped onion

3 tomatoes, coarsely chopped

2 fresh green jalapeño or serrano chilies, seeded and finely chopped

1 bunch cilantro leaves, coarsely chopped

4 lemons

sea salt and freshly ground black pepper

1 Preheat the oven to 400°F (200°C). Clean the inside of the fish and season with salt and pepper, a little of the garlic, and some of the spices, rubbing inside and out. Heat a heavy frying pan over medium-high heat and add a little oil. Cook the fish quickly on both sides until golden brown. Carefully lift from the pan and place in an ovenproof dish.

2 Add a little extra oil to the same frying pan, and cook the remaining garlic and spices. Add the onion and tomato. Add most of the chopped cilantro, the green chilies, and the juice of 3 of the lemons. Cook for 3–4 minutes. Stuff the fish with the onion mixture; spoon any remaining mixture over the fish. Cover with foil and bake in the oven for 20–25 minutes until cooked through, depending upon the size of the fish. To check, insert a fork into the dense meat at the back of the head. If the meat is white and flaky, the fish is done. (Remember, when a piece of fish or meat is taken from the oven, it will continue to cook from the residual heat.)

3 To serve, garnish with the remaining chopped cilantro and the juice of the remaining lemon. The spices, green chilies, and lemon work together to cut the richness of the fish. This dish is delicious whether eaten hot, warm, or cold, accompanied by freshly cooked vegetables and salads, and freshly-baked bread.

Kofte kebab Lamb kebabs with white bean and tomato salad

Serves 4–6

2 garlic cloves, halved

a little olive oil

1 onion, finely chopped

2 tsp ground cumin

2 tsp paprika

1 tsp cayenne pepper

1lb (450g) ground lamb

handful of flat-leaf parsley leaves,
   coarsely chopped

handful of fresh cilantro leaves,
   coarsely chopped

½ cup unsalted pistachio nuts,
   coarsely chopped

sea salt and freshly ground black pepper

For the salad

1 cup dried cannellini beans

2 garlic cloves, peeled but left whole

½ bunch of flat-leaf parsley, leaves picked
   and chopped (stalks reserved)

3 tbsp red wine vinegar

3 tbsp extra virgin olive oil

1 tsp ground cumin

2 ripe tomatoes, cut into ½in (1cm) dice

I had this fantastic variation of a spicy kofte, or kofte kebab, in the spring in Istanbul. I ate them in view of the mighty Bosphorus. The rich, juicy meat was very well spiced with cumin and paprika, and studded throughout with bright green pistachios. When you cut into the meat, the nuts glistened like shining jewels. The kebabs here are smaller than the traditional long kofte kebab, so you may want to use short bamboo skewers. Or simply make small meatballs if you prefer, flattening them slightly once they are in the pan.

1 To make the salad, soak the beans overnight in a large bowl of cold water. Drain and rinse under cold running water. Put into a large heavy pot, and cover with fresh cold water. Add the garlic, reserved parsley stalks, and a splash of olive oil. Do not add salt. Bring to a boil, reduce the heat, and simmer for 1 hour 20 minutes to 1 hour 40 minutes, or until the beans are tender but still slightly firm to the bite. Drain off the liquid. Stir in the vinegar, extra virgin olive oil, and cumin to the beans. Season well with salt and pepper. Let sit for about 20 minutes to blend the flavors. Stir in the tomatoes and parsley just before serving.

2 To make the kebabs, soak the bamboo skewers in cold water for at least 30 minutes so they do not burn. Crush the garlic with a little salt to make a paste. Heat a little oil in a heavy frying pan over medium-high heat. Cook the onion for 4 minutes or until soft. Add the garlic, cumin, paprika, and cayenne, and cook for a couple of minutes longer, or until fragrant. Remove from the heat, transfer to a bowl, and let cool for 5 minutes. Add the lamb, parsley, cilantro, and pistachios. Season well. Mold the lamb mixture onto one end of the skewer, making a cylinder of meat around roughly half its length. Heat a little oil in a large heavy frying pan over medium-high heat. Cook the kofte kebabs in batches until golden brown all over. Drain on paper towels. Serve with the salad and lots of fresh crusty bread.

Salatet bil s'banegh joz
Spinach and walnut salad

Serves 4

2 tbsp extra virgin olive oil	½ cup Greek-style yogurt
1 onion, finely chopped	20 fresh mint leaves, coarsely chopped
½lb (225g) fresh spinach leaves, rinsed, stems discarded, and coarsely chopped	seeds of ½ pomegranate (see method on p36)
¼ cup walnut halves and pieces	salt and freshly ground black pepper
1 garlic clove, finely chopped	

1 Heat the olive oil in a heavy frying pan over medium-high heat, and cook the onion for 4–5 minutes until pale golden. Add the spinach and stir for a couple of minutes to wilt. Remove from the heat. In a separate pan, dry-roast the walnuts over medium-high heat for a few minutes, then coarsely chop. Crush the garlic with a little salt and add to the yogurt.

2 Season the spinach with salt and black pepper. Drain off any excess liquid and place on a serving dish. Pour the yogurt and garlic mixture over the top. Scatter with walnuts and mint, and garnish with the pomegranate seeds.

This is another deliciously simple mezze that could be eaten at the beginning of the meal with other dishes to follow. What often happens when eating in this way in the Middle East is that the small dishes and plates stay on the table, even when the next course of meat arrives. It is a seamless, continuous flow of food arriving at the table. This dish is a perfect combination of flavors and textures—the sourness of pomegranate and yogurt complement the earthy flavor of the walnuts. It could also be served as a salad on its own or alongside some grilled meat, fish, or chicken.

Lohz Spiced roast almonds

Serves 6–8 with drinks

3 tbsp sunflower oil	½ tsp ground chili powder
1½ cups whole blanched almonds	½ cup brown sugar
1 tsp ground cumin	juice of ½ lemon
1 tsp ground cinnamon	salt and freshly ground black pepper

1 Preheat the oven to 300°F (150°C). Heat a heavy frying pan over medium-high heat. Add the oil, almonds, cumin, cinnamon, chili powder, and two-thirds of the brown sugar. Toss the nuts in the sugar to coat thoroughly. Continue to sauté until the nuts are caramelized and the sugar has melted. Stir in the lemon juice and remove from the heat.

2 Transfer the nuts to a bowl, and season well with salt and pepper, stirring to mix. Spread the nuts on a baking sheet and bake for 5 minutes, just to let them dry out. Sprinkle with the remaining brown sugar to taste.

3 Serve warm or at room temperature. They will keep in a clean, dry airtight container for a couple of weeks without spoiling.

Grinding and refreshing spices Grinding your own spices from whole pods and seeds is so simple it is worth making this a habit. The reward far outweighs any extra time and effort involved, as freshly ground spices have much better flavor and aroma than store-bought versions do. Invest in an electric coffee grinder or a wooden one that has a small drawer. Grind a batch as small or as large as you want, then sieve to get rid of any tough husks. (Don't make too large a batch if you are not going to be using it within a relatively short period of time, as it will only become stale.) Store the spice mixture in an airtight glass jar with a tight-fitting lid, and use as needed. To refresh ground spices, place the quantity that you want to use in a dry frying pan or skillet, and heat over low-medium heat for a couple of minutes until the spice becomes fragrant.

Nuts and seeds feature in many dishes throughout the Levant and along the North African coast, from mezze and snacks, to main courses and desserts. With each nut stall or trader come family recipes and spice mixes passed down over generations. In the scented passages of the souk in Damascus I happened upon an ingenious portable nut stall that was a customized bicycle. At the front where a basket would have been was a flat hotplate heated underneath with charcoal. This ensured that the nuts were freshly roasted in small batches. The bike came complete with a six-foot metal chimney.

Kara'a Libyan pumpkin dip

Serves 6

1lb (450g) pumpkin, peeled, seeded, and
   flesh cut into 1in (2cm) cubes

1 tsp caraway seeds

1 tsp cumin seeds

3 garlic cloves, finely chopped

1 fresh red jalapeño or serrano chili, seeded
   and finely chopped

juice of 1 lemon

¼–½ cup extra virgin olive oil

salt and freshly ground black pepper

1 Place the pumpkin in a saucepan with ½ cup water and simmer, partially covered, for about 10 minutes or until soft. Season well with salt and pepper. Drain. Mash the pumpkin with a fork until smooth. Set aside.

2 Dry-roast the caraway and cumin seeds in a small frying pan over medium-high heat for a couple of minutes until fragrant. Crush the toasted seeds using a pestle and mortar. Add the garlic, chili, and a pinch of salt, and work into a smooth paste. Add the spice mixture to the pumpkin along with the lemon juice. Mix, then stir in enough olive oil to make a dipping consistency. Serve either hot or cold as part of a mezze, accompanied by lots of hot pita bread.

Throughout the Middle East, dips and pastes are eaten as part of a larger selection of mezze. Lots of them are vegetable-based, a light and healthy option compared to the often richer meat-based main courses. This dip makes a change from some of the more common ones such as hummus. The chili and spices provide a peppery heat, contrasting with the pumpkin's sweetness. Try butternut squash, sweet potato, or beets in place of the pumpkin. The vegetables could also be roasted, then puréed, to give added depth of flavor to the finished dip.

Muhammara Spiced tomato relish

Serves 6–8

2 red bell peppers	2 garlic cloves, halved
¾ cup walnuts	1 tsp cayenne pepper
¾ cup hazelnuts	1 tsp ground cumin
10 cherry tomatoes, halved	1 tbsp pomegranate molasses
1 fresh red jalapeño or serrano chili, seeded	½ cup olive oil
and finely chopped	juice of 1 lemon

1 Heat a grill pan or broiler until very hot. Grill the peppers, turning often, until the skin is blistered and charred on all sides. Transfer to a bowl and cover tightly with plastic wrap. (The trapped moisture makes it easier to peel off the blackened skin.) When cool enough to handle, peel off and discard the skin; then halve and remove any seeds and membrane. Coarsely chop the flesh.

2 Process the walnuts and hazelnuts in a food processor until finely ground. Add the bell pepper, tomatoes, chili, garlic, cayenne, cumin, and pomegranate molasses. Work into a smooth paste. With the motor running, gradually add the oil in a thin, steady stream, as if you were making a mayonnaise. If the mixture gets too thick, add a little of the lemon juice. Once all the oil has been incorporated, process in the remaining lemon juice.

3 Serve at room temperature as a dip with lots of hot fresh pita bread, or as one of many dishes as part of a mezze selection. If making in advance, refrigerate until needed. It will keep up to 5 days, and over time the flavors will only become more vibrant.

I had pastes similar to this in Syria, Turkey, and Lebanon. They are left on the table so that they can accompany soups and grilled meats. In Syria and Turkey, this spicy red sauce is called "muhammara," which means "made red." Some pastes contain walnuts; others use roast hazelnuts. Red peppers or tomatoes, or both, can be used to sweeten the paste and bulk it up. However it is made, this paste is packed with spicy fire and is addictively delicious. It works particularly well when the flavors are allowed to develop overnight or even for a few days in the refrigerator.

Tarator bi tahini Sesame tarator sauce

Serves 6 as part of a mezze selection

2 garlic cloves

½ tsp salt

large pinch of cayenne pepper

1 cup (8oz) tahini (sesame seed paste)

½ cup good-quality olive oil

⅔ cup fresh lemon juice

salt and freshly ground black pepper

1 Crush the garlic cloves with the back of a heavy knife on a board. Add the salt and cayenne pepper. Continue to work until you have a smooth paste.

2 Transfer the garlic paste to a bowl, and whisk continuously while slowly pouring in the tahini and olive oil, as if you were making a mayonnaise. If the mixture gets too thick, thin with a little lemon juice, then continue the process. Once all the tahini and olive oil have been incorporated, add the remaining lemon juice. Taste the sauce and season with a little salt and pepper if necessary.

Note If the nut flavor is too overpowering, try whisking a little yogurt into the mixture, which softens the intensity.

Tarator bi sonoba (pine nut tarator sauce) Remove the crust from 2 slices white bread. Soak the bread in a little milk until soft. Crush 2 peeled garlic cloves with the back of a heavy knife on a board. Add ½ tsp salt and a large pinch of cayenne pepper. Work until smooth. Place the paste in a food processor with 2 cups pine nuts and process until finely chopped. Add the soaked bread and any excess milk. Continue to process, gradually adding ½ cup oil in a thin, steady stream, as if you were making a mayonnaise. Thin the sauce with the juice of 2 lemons. Taste and season with salt and freshly ground black pepper. This delicious sauce complements grilled meat, fish, and vegetables. You could use a combination of nuts such as almonds or walnuts to get a more complex depth of flavor, or roast some of them before grinding to create more contrast.

This sauce is used often in Middle Eastern food, served with hot and cold vegetable dishes, as well as falafel or as part of a mezze table. It is most often served cold; however, in one small market café by the coast in Lebanon, I had a delicious dish where fresh firm fillets of white fish were first grilled, then coated in this tahini sauce with lots of chopped parsley, and finally baked in the oven. The sweet fresh fish was a great contrast to the intense lemony, nutty sauce. Another version, tarator bi sonoba, is made with pine nuts; the recipe for this is also given.

Ablama
Zucchini stuffed with lamb and pine nuts

Serves 6

2lb (900g) small zucchini	1¼lb (550g) ground lamb
½ cup olive oil	¾ cup pine nuts
2 garlic cloves, finely chopped	3 ripe tomatoes
½ tsp ground cumin	30 flat-leaf parsley leaves, coarsely chopped
½ tsp ground cloves	juice of 1 lemon
½ tsp ground cinnamon	1 cup good-quality chicken stock
1 onion, finely chopped	salt and freshly ground black pepper

I had these delicious spiced zucchini in a small café in Damascus in Syria. They are definitely worth the bit of fuss that is needed to make them. The key is to get small firm zucchini at the beginning of the season, as opposed to massive watery ones that are mostly seeds inside. There is also an alternative preparation method. Simply cut the zucchini in half lengthwise, then scrape out all the seeds using a small spoon. Each half is then stuffed with the filling. The zucchini are still fried, but you do not turn them over; otherwise the meat stuffing will fall out!

1 Cut the tops off the zucchini and, using a small spoon or melon baller, hollow out the inside of each.

2 Heat 1 tbsp of the olive oil in a heavy frying pan over medium-high heat. Cook the garlic, cumin, cloves, and cinnamon for a couple of minutes until fragrant. Add the onion and cook until soft and pale golden, then add the lamb. Continue cooking until all the liquid has evaporated, breaking up and stirring the lamb around the pan to brown evenly. Season well with salt and pepper. Mix in the pine nuts. Taste and adjust the seasoning.

3 Cut a cross in the bottom of the tomatoes and, using the tip of a small sharp knife, remove the core from each one. Blanch in boiling water for 10 seconds, then refresh in cold water. Peel off the skin and discard. Cut the tomatoes in half, remove the seeds, and cut the flesh into a small dice. Set aside.

4 Using a small spoon, stuff the zucchini with the lamb mixture, pushing the filling down into each zucchini so it is plump with stuffing. Heat the remaining oil, and cook the zucchini, turning, until soft. Cook in batches while continuing to stuff the remainder of the zucchini.

5 Mix the diced tomato with the parsley, and season with salt and pepper. Add the lemon juice and chicken stock. Place the cooked zucchini in a flameproof dish. Pour the tomato mixture over the top, and cook over medium heat until the sauce is hot. Serve with rice or bread. This dish works particularly well with a selection of other mezze dishes, with lots of hot bread to soak up all the good cooking juices.

Houmous bil erfeh lahem
Hummus with cinnamon lamb

This is a fresh version of hummus without the strong flavor of the sesame that comes from the tahini. There are a number of variations of hummus: some are smooth; others have a more coarse texture. This one uses dried chilies and cayenne pepper to give a great warmth that works very well with the fried lamb and the other spices. Alternatively, leave out the spices and add lots of freshly chopped parsley and cilantro instead. It can be served without the fried lamb, but this combination is typical of the small cafés in Beirut and Lebanon.

Serves 6

2 garlic cloves

¼ tsp crushed dried red chilies

1 (15oz) can chickpeas (garbanzo beans), drained and rinsed

2 tbsp extra virgin olive oil

½ tsp cayenne pepper

small handful of flat-leaf parsley, plus extra, coarsely chopped, for garnish

3 tbsp lemon juice

1 tbsp Greek-style yogurt

2 tbsp sunflower oil

¼lb (115g) ground or minced lamb

1 tsp ground cinnamon

salt and freshly ground black pepper

chopped toasted almonds or walnuts, to garnish (optional)

1 To make the hummus, crush the garlic with the dried chili flakes and a little salt until you have a smooth paste. In the bowl of a food processor, combine the rinsed chickpeas with the garlic paste and olive oil and process until almost smooth. Using a spatula, push all the mixture down from the sides of the bowl before adding the cayenne pepper, parsley, and lemon juice. Season with salt and pepper, and add the yogurt. With the motor running, gradually add the sunflower oil in a thin, steady stream until you have a smooth light paste. (If you want a slightly thinner consistency, simply add a little water.)

2 Heat a frying pan over medium-high heat, add a little oil, and cook the lamb until brown and crispy. Sprinkle over the cinnamon and season well with salt and pepper. Stir through well.

3 Spoon the lamb into a well in the center of the chickpea purée, and sprinkle with the extra chopped parsley. This is a delicious sauce that complements grilled meat, fish, or vegetables. If desired, garnish with chopped toasted almonds or walnuts.

Shawi ras el hanut ghanmi
Spicy lamb chops

Serves 4–6

4 tbsp (½ stick) unsalted butter, cut
  into pieces

½ tsp ground coriander

½ tsp ground nutmeg

1 tsp ground ginger

½ tsp ground cardamom

large pinch of ground cloves

½ tsp ground Lebanese spice
  mix (see p218)

2 garlic cloves, crushed

30 cilantro leaves, chopped

30 mint leaves, chopped

juice of 1 lemon

12 lamb loin chops, trimmed of excess fat

salt and freshly ground black pepper

1 Gently melt the butter in a small saucepan over medium heat. Add the spices and cook for 2–3 minutes until fragrant. Add the garlic, cilantro, and mint. Mix well, then season with salt and pepper. Add the lemon juice and remove from the heat. Let sit in a warm place for at least 1 hour to blend flavors.

2 Heat an outdoor grill, grill pan, or broiler until very hot. Season the lamb with salt and pepper, then brush with the spicy butter. When the grill has reached a high heat, cook the lamb for 4–5 minutes on each side, continuing to baste frequently with the butter to keep the meat moist and impart flavor. (Infusing the spices in a warm place so that all the flavors blend and then basting frequently are the keys to making this dish a rousing success.) Grill until the meat is brown and crispy on the outside, but still pink and juicy on the inside. Let the chops rest 3–5 minutes before serving at once.

This spice mixture bears similarities to a tandoor recipe from India and demonstrates the way in which ingredients follow much the same migration patterns as people, as well as displaying the influences that have passed from one part of the Muslim world to another. If you grind the spices yourself from whole, you achieve a much more aromatic result. Buy an electric coffee grinder just for spices. You can then grind your spices in order to make your own blends. You could use this recipe for lamb steaks, chicken drumsticks or skewers, or pork or beef to great effect.

Luz biskwi
Almond and cardamom biscuits

Makes 20–30 biscuits

2 cups flour

2½ tbsp cold unsalted butter, cut
   into chunks

1 tbsp orange flower water

⅔ cup almonds, cooked in a small amount
   of oil until golden; drained and then ground

3 green cardamom pods

sugar to taste

vegetable oil for deep-frying

These simple-to-make little biscuits work very well with a strong cup of coffee or some fresh mint tea. The flavor combination of cardamom, orange flower water, and roasted nuts is very emotive of the Middle East and conjures up images of spice markets, silks, and artifacts. These treats are delicious with a cream- or milk-based dessert such as panna cotta or Turkish rice pudding. You could use a different sort of nut such as pistachios or hazelnuts, and cinnamon or nutmeg can be substituted for the cardamom.

1 Sift the flour into a large bowl, and rub the butter into the flour with your fingertips until the mixture is the texture of breadcrumbs. Add the orange flower water and a little cold water, just enough to make a smooth, soft dough. Cut the dough into small pieces, and open them out with your index finger and thumb so you have uneven, semi-flattened shapes. Heat 1in (2.5cm) or more of vegetable oil in a saucepan over medium heat until very hot. Fry the biscuits in small batches for a few minutes until golden brown. Drain on paper towels.

2 Using a pestle and mortar, first grind the roasted almonds, then the cardamom pods. Mix the almonds, cardamom, and some sugar together, and toss the fried dough pieces in the mixture until coated. Serve warm or at room temperature, as a snack or with coffee or tea, or alongside a milk or cream dessert such as good-quality ice cream or a custard.

The Menus

The Menus

Despite the enormous variety and diversity of street food from many countries, there are some common threads that run throughout. One of them is the communal nature of how the food is eaten. The food, the condiments, and the whole experience are shared by groups of friends and family—from eating some *mezze* in the Middle East to enjoying *chaat* in South India. People meet after work and before they head home, sharing contrasting dishes to create an intimate occasion. Alternatively, large groups can often be found eating en masse from the same stall.

I found one such example of this phenomenon in Salvador de Bahia in the northeast of Brazil. A dish with virtual cult status in this baroque city is *acaraje*. These delicious spicy bean patties are eaten late in the evening by hundreds of people at various stalls, before they all head out to party the night away in true Brazilian fashion. One particular stall that I visited was situated on the corner of a large square. There was seating for about 400 people in all, and the place was packed. The *acaraje* and their traditional accompaniments of salty dried prawns and hot and sour salad came from just that single stall. The surrounding cafés and bars were providing the beers, coconut juice, and other drinks, and at midnight the place was jumping. I had similar "mass-market" experiences of street food many times during my research for the book. What these experiences of delicious food from all over the world showed me was the importance of sharing food with friends. The shared experience of street food, of passing plates and eating together, encourages personal connections, and I wanted to create a menu section to show how this could be done for different occasions. There are so many types and styles of street food that can be eaten at any time of the day or night. They will work for picnics, barbecues, or those occasions when you are serving food without plates, such as canapé and cocktail parties. Street food can be used for light lunches or cozy nights in, or for more formal dinner parties. Depending on the complexity of the event, there are dishes that can happily be used for each.

In this section, I have put together groups from the same region and also from further afield, but which use similar principles of cooking or may have some complementary or contrasting flavors. These menus are a simple guide, to show how a number of dishes can be combined to entice and satisfy your guests. I encourage you to be creative and experiment with your own choices for special meals to be shared with friends or family. Dipping into the bounty of delicious choices from different cuisines, and putting them in the context of entertaining at home, brings its own rewards and will satisfy both the appetite and the imagination.

Picnic

Street food is great for a picnic because it is very easy to transport, and the basket will be much lighter on the return journey because everything will have been eaten with no waste. Whether you are meeting in the park, on the beach, on a hilltop, or at the races, the delectable contents of your basket will prove the envy of all around because of its culinary diversity. A picnic made up of street food specialities will be much more memorable than some sandy cheese sandwiches or plain cold chicken. Instead, conjure up images of Mediterranean holidays, ancient spice routes, and oriental feasts. Pack your food, don't forget your refreshing drinks and fresh crusty bread, and most of all enjoy your day.

Menu 1

Potato, sausage, and sun-dried tomato pizza Italy pp136–137

Carrot and orange salad Morocco pp170–171

Libyan pumpkin dip Libya pp182–183

Hummus with cinnamon lamb Lebanon pp188–189

Harissa mini fish cakes with preserved lemon Morocco pp150–151

Menu 2

Grilled scallions wrapped in pancetta Italy pp116–117

Flat bread, pumpkin paste, carrot pickle Afghanistan pp152–155

Poussin stuffed with olives, onion, and rosemary Italy pp120–121

Zucchini salad Morocco p158

Date pastries Malta pp138–139

The food used for a picnic is very pick-up-able, and you will not need an excess of plates, knives, or forks. Spread out the contents of your hamper, and enjoy impressing your friends with bright colors, contrasting textures, and delicious flavors.

Menu 3

Savory ricotta-filled pastries Malta pp118–119

Lamb kebabs with tomato and white bean salad Turkey pp176–177

Green tomato salsa with chorizo in a tortilla Mexico pp104–105

Toasted pita bread salad Lebanon pp156–157

Sweet fried ravioli Italy pp122–123

Menu 4

Spinach pastries Lebanon pp164–165

Grilled tuna, sprouting broccoli, and ricotta calzone Italy p135

Barbecued jerk chicken with pineapple salsa Jamaica pp92–93

Spiced tomato relish Turkey p184

Spiced roast almonds Syria pp180–181

Top right: Potato, sausage, and sun-dried
tomato pizza; bottom left: Carrot and orange salad

Barbecue

From Turkey to Singapore, Ecuador to Vietnam, many street food dishes are grilled on outside barbecues and grills. The methods of grilling vary as much as the ingredients, marinades, spice rubs, and recipes. Street food lends itself very well to the home or portable barbecue, and it is perfect for summer evenings or lazy weekends. Aromatic plumes of smoke often guided me to stalls selling delicious items that epitomized the countries that I visited. I smelled where I was going long before I saw the meat, fish, cheese, or vegetable ready to be devoured with the aid of nothing more than a pile of crumpled paper napkins. Anticipation of the food to be eaten creates a great sense of atmosphere. Your guests will be salivating.

The beauty of a barbecue is that, even though the preparation, marinating, and lighting of the thing may take some time, the actual cooking of the food is quick, and the results are instantly gratifying.

Menu 1

Grilled salty cheese marinated with oregano Brazil pp88–89

Spicy lamb chops Morocco pp190–191

Grilled artichokes with garlic, chili, and pine nuts Italy pp128–129

Fresh peach salsa Mexico pp94–95

Green cashew nut sauce Brazil p107

Menu 2

Summer rolls Vietnam pp44–45

Mango, papaya, and pineapple salad Singapore pp58–59

Chinese barbecued pork China pp66–67

Skewers of beef with green chili sauce Thailand pp62–63

Hot and sour squid and green mango salad Vietnam pp68–69

Menu 3

Chaat with green chili and pomegranate India pp36–37

Seared steak with chimichurri Argentina p97

Spiced grilled chicken with coconut cream Malaysia pp76–77

Zucchini salad Morocco p158

Sweet potato and pumpkin doughnuts Ecuador pp98–99

Menu 4

Grilled scallions wrapped in pancetta Italy pp116–117

Lamb kebabs with white bean and tomato salad Turkey pp176–177

Grilled sardines Turkey pp144–145

Sesame salad Syria p159

Green tomato salsa Mexico pp104–105

Top right: Fresh peach salsa; bottom left: Grilled salty cheese marinated with oregano; bottom right: Spicy lamb chops

Leisurely lunch

The sharing of street food really brings the community together. In countries in the Middle East and Southeast Asia, you will often see family and friends all enjoying street food dishes as a group. The party may span several generations, from revered great-grandparents to the youngest additions to the family clan. Sharing different dishes of street food makes for a very informal, relaxed type of meal; it is the food that brings everyone together. There is something for everyone to dip into while catching up on each other's lives. Different textures and flavors build a colorful mixture of contrasts—much like the family or friends who are enjoying the meal.

Menu 1

Chard soup with rice and turmeric Jordan pp148–149

Hot and sour grilled beef salad Vietnam pp72–73

Lamb meatballs with sour cherry sauce Turkey pp162–163

Smoky roast eggplant dip Lebanon p168

Sweet fried ravioli Italy pp122–123

Menu 2

Chicken-stuffed flat bread with curry sauce Singapore pp46–48

Eastern jeweled pilaf Jordan pp160–161

Salad of roast pork with cucumber Vietnam pp78–79

Hummus with cinnamon lamb Lebanon pp188–189

Toasted pita bread salad Lebanon pp154–155

Some of the best food in the world is the simplest and eaten by the people who have the least. Peasant and street food cooks from all over the world have to be much more resourceful to create delicious food because they do not have luxury ingredients at their disposal. You can apply similar principles to an informal lunch, where the food should be simple yet packed full of flavor.

Menu 3

Salt cod croquettes Spain pp130–131

Coriander marinated fish Morocco pp174–175

Potato and cumin curry India pp38–39

Spinach and walnut salad Syria pp176–177

Almond and cardamom biscuits Morocco pp192–193

Menu 4

Spicy mussel soup Brazil pp86–87

Crispy paratha India pp34–35

Spicy fried okra Sri Lanka pp32–33

Zucchini stuffed with lamb and pine nuts Syria pp186–187

Yogurt cream cheese dip Lebanon p169

Top left: Hot and sour grilled beef salad; bottom left: Smoky roast eggplant dip; bottom right: Lamb meatballs with sour cherry sauce

Cozy night in

Street food is often thought of simply as snacks eaten with the fingers, but there are also much more elaborate dishes that constitute a whole meal. When transported into your home, they provide something completely different than the fare found at your average dinner party. If you like, serve the dishes in a continuous stream, as they are prepared. This is similar to the Asian style of eating where there is really no break and definition between courses. It is a very relaxed way of dining, as each guest has a bowl or small plate, and chooses whatever he or she wants to eat. The meal is not rushed, with breaks between dishes while another dish is prepared, leaving time for chatting. Your guests will definitely be impressed.

Menu 1

Spicy bean soup Morocco pp166–167

Marinated quail with caper sauce Italy pp132–133

Eastern jeweled pilaf Jordan pp160–161

Spinach and walnut salad Syria pp176–177

Pumpkin pudding Brazil pp108–109

Menu 2

Mexican pumpkin flower soup Mexico pp100–101

Pan-fried red mullet Italy pp124–125

Stuffed eggplant with yogurt and pine nuts Lebanon p146

Carrot and orange salad Morocco pp170–171

Date pastries Malta pp138–139

Menu 3

Coconut and turmeric fish soup Sri Lanka pp26–27

Potato and cumin curry India pp38–39

Paper-wrapped chicken Malaysia pp52–53

Fresh cilantro and peanut chutney Sri Lanka p31

Sichuan-style vegetable stir-fry China pp54–55

Menu 4

Spicy seasoned potato in a cone India pp28–30

Stuffed fish balls Lebanon p147

Grilled artichokes with garlic, chili, and pine nuts Italy pp128–129

Bean patties with avocado and tomato salad Brazil pp90–91

Honey and nut pastries Italy pp126–127

For a different approach, take your guests on an undulating journey of contrasting tastes in the form of small courses that do not leave you too full at the end of the meal. You could match each course with a different wine to make a really special event.

Top left: Spicy bean soup; top right: Marinated quail
with caper sauce; bottom right: Pumpkin pudding

Cocktail party

Street food can work very well in the form of finger food or canapés for cocktail parties. The key to this sort of food is to ensure the right balance of the four main flavors of hot, sweet, salty, and sour in one mouthful. Several food styles can be represented without confusion, and the food can emerge from the kitchen throughout the evening, as hot and fresh as from the best street food stalls. What also works brilliantly is having a combination of different sorts of foods that are all fully flavored, but of varying complexity. Dips and pastes, for example, are delicious but very simple to put together. Instead of going for more elaborate dishes, serve the rustic choices that will still impress your guests.

When it comes to displaying finger food for your guests' eating pleasure, arrange individual items in odd numbers. If there are three or five of any one thing on a serving plate or platter, your eyes and fingers are drawn to them because they look interesting and imperfect. If the numbers are even, people hesitate to spoil the symmetry.

Menu 1

Masala popadums with tomato and green chili India pp24–25

Indonesian beef saté skewers Indonesia p49

Lebanese lamb pizza Lebanon pp172–173

Harissa mini fish cakes with preserved lemon Morocco pp150–151

Savory ricotta-filled pastries Malta pp118–119

Menu 2

Spicy seasoned potato in a cone India pp28–30

Seafood empanadas Ecuador pp102–103

Crispy chicken spring rolls Vietnam pp60–61

Semolina flour fritters Italy pp114–115

Libyan pumpkin dip Libya pp182–183

Menu 3

Paper-wrapped chicken Malaysia pp52–53

Prawn fritters with sweet chili sauce Singapore pp56–57

Potato, sausage, and sun-dried tomato pizza Italy pp136–137

Spiced tomato relish Turkey p184

Spinach pastries Lebanon pp164–165

Menu 4

Summer rolls Vietnam pp46–47

Chaat with green chili and pomegranate India pp36–37

Skewers of beef with green chili sauce Thailand pp62–63

Salt cod croquettes Spain pp130–131

Spiced roast almonds Syria pp180–181

Top left: Indonesian beef saté skewers;
bottom right: Masala popadums with tomato and green chili

Glossary

bok choy Part of the Brassica family, bok choy is also known as Chinese white cabbage and white mustard cabbage. It is used in salads and stir-fries.

Chinese cabbage Also called napa cabbage, celery cabbage, and Peking cabbage, Chinese cabbage is part of the mustard family. Not to be confused with bok choy, it is used in salads and stir-fries.

chipotle Chipotles are dried and smoked ripe jalapeño chiles. Commonly used throughout Mexico, chipotles are available in several forms: as a powder, as whole dried chipotle pods, in a can as *chipotle en adobo* (combined with other spices as a paste), or as a concentrated paste. Chipotles are available from Latin American grocers or gourmet food stores.

choy sum Another member of the cabbage family, choy sum is also called flowering white cabbage and Chinese flowering cabbage. It is used in salads and stir-fries, and is available from Asian and Chinese grocers, and better greengrocers.

daikon Also known as mooli, Japanese radish, Chinese radish, or Oriental radish, this long root vegetable has crisp white flesh; the skin is either creamy white or black.

Look for daikon with unwrinkled skin. It can be used raw in salads or as a garnish, or cooked in stir-fries. It is available from Indian, Asian, and Japanese grocers.

fish sauce This pungent liquid made from fermented anchovies or other fish is an essential Southeast Asian ingredient. It loses its fishiness on cooking, mellowing to add flavor. Recipes vary, but can be used interchangeably. Known as nam pla in Thailand and nuoc nam in Vietnam, it is available from good supermarkets and Asian grocers.

galangal Especially popular in Thai cuisine, galangal is a hot and peppery aromatic rhizome. A little like ginger root, it is used as a seasoning throughout Southeast Asia. It is available in both root and dried forms from Asian grocers.

harissa This fiery paste made from chiles, garlic, and spices is available in supermarkets and Middle Eastern markets. It can be bought in a tube which looks like tomato paste, or in cans or jars; you can also buy it as a dry spice mix and make your own with the addition of tomato paste, lemon, and salt.

masa harina This flour is ground from corn kernels that have first been soaked in lime water, then dried. This is the process that makes it differ from ordinary cornmeal. *Masa* is traditionally used

to make corn tortillas. *Masa harina* is used in Central and South American cooking, and is available from Latin American grocers.

Lebanese spice mix This term can be quite ambiguous, as each chef has his or her personal recipe. A guideline is 4 parts ground cinnamon, 1 part ground cloves, 1 part chili powder, and 1 part ground cardamom. Grind your own using a clean coffee grinder, store in an airtight jar, and use as needed.

palm oil Extracted from the fruit of the African palm, this reddish-orange oil is very high in saturated fats. Commonly used in Brazilian cooking, especially in Bahia, it has a distinctive flavor and should not be mistaken for the milder and lighter palm kernel oil.

palm sugar This sugar is made from the sap of date or coconut palms. It is also known as coconut sugar, gur, and jaggery. In India, the term *jaggery* also refers to sugar made from raw sugarcane.

pimentón Pimentón is a smoked paprika and comes in two varieties: *pimentón dulce* (sweet and mild) and *pimentón picante* (hot). It is available from good supermarkets and Latin American grocers.

pomegranate molasses A fantastic Middle Eastern ingredient, pomegranate molasses comes in bottles. A thick, dark syrup made from the reduced juice of puréed pomegranates, it is fabulously sour and sweet at the same time, similar to very good quality aged balsamic vinegar. If not available, substitute a little reduced balsamic vinegar.

queijo de coalho A Brazilian cheese, *queijo de coalho* is similar in taste and texture to haloumi, which works well as an alternative.

sambal oelek A *sambal* is a spicy and fiery paste made primarily from chiles and is often served as a condiment. Used in Southeast Asian cooking, particularly in Indonesia, Singapore, and Malaysia, there are several forms. One is *sambal oelek* (perhaps the most basic), which is made with chiles, brown sugar, and salt. It is available in jars from Asian grocers.

shrimp paste Made from salted fermented prawns, shrimp paste comes in a block and has a pungent smell and strong taste, which dissipates on cooking to become aromatic. Recipes vary slightly depending on the country in which it is made. It should be used only sparingly and is available from Asian grocers.

sour cherry The sour cherry (*Prunus cerasus*) is smaller than its sweet counterpart, and comes in several varieties, including Aleppo, Montmorency, and Morello. Fresh

sour cherries are usually available from late spring to early summer. Fresh sour cherries from the Aleppo region can be difficult to come by unless you have a good Middle Eastern grocer nearby. Dried sour cherries are a perfect substitute and are found in good supermarkets.

sumac A dark red berry, sumac is dried and ground into a coarse powder that can be almost purple in color and has a very distinctive peppery, sour, and slightly bitter flavor. Commonly used in cooking of the Levant and Middle East, it is treated as a condiment like pepper. It is available from Middle Eastern grocers and health-food stores. If you cannot find it, use lots of black pepper and lemon juice in its place.

tamarind This is an essential ingredient in Indian and Southeast Asian cooking, and is also found in Middle Eastern and Persian recipes. The fruit of the tamarind are large pods yielding both seeds and a tart pulp. Used as a flavoring in much the same way as lemon juice, the pulp comes in concentrated form in jars, as a paste, in a dried brick, or as a powder. It is available from Indian, Asian, and some Middle Eastern grocers.

Thai basil This has a different flavor from ordinary basil and is similar to anise. If not available, substitute a combination of fresh cilantro and mint leaves.

Useful websites

India and Sri Lanka

http://store.indianfoodsco.com

http://www.kalustyans.com

http://www.qualityspices.com

China and Southeast Asia

http://www.asiafoods.com

http://www.importfood.com

http://www.asianfoodgrocer.com

Latin America and the Caribbean

http://www.mexgrocer.com

http://www.latinmerchant.com

http://www.caribimports.com

Middle East and North Africa

http://www.daynasmarket.com

http://www.eturkuaz.com

http://www.tasteofturkey.com

http://www.belazu.com

General

http://www.ethnicfoodsco.com

http://store.asianfoodcompany.com

http://www.penzeys.com

Index

Acknowledgments

Author

Thank you to Mary-Clare Jerram, Carl Raymond, and Monika Schlitzer for seeing the potential in my writing. To Borra Garson and Martine Carter at Deborah McKenna Ltd. Thank you to Dawn Henderson, Siobhán O'Connor, Susan Downing, Simon Daley, and Julia Kepinska, and the fantastic teams at DK. Thank you to Lisa Linder for her spectacular photographs and Alice Hart for making such delicious food, and to Jasmine Hart for growing (and delivering) the pumpkin flowers.

Huge appreciation to the people around the world who so generously helped in my pursuit of this book. First to Heather Paterson, who makes my life work, and Toni Vallenduuk of Flight Centre. In Ecuador, Alegría Plaza, Maria Clara Perez and her family, Marita Uribe, and Fernando Perez; from Argentina, Alicia and Jose Quo Sada, Hugh and Celina Arnold; the Brazilians for showing me such a good time, Silvania Presta, Bec and Michel Saad, Gabi Kropacsy and her mum for showing me the real samba in Rio. Stuart Campbell and Bina Shah for their contacts. Sara Grasso for showing me culinary Sicily. In Malta, big thanks to Michael Zammit Tobana, owner of the Fortina Spa Resort, and to the chefs at Taste, at the Fortina, who cook my food so well. A massive thank you to Ratnesh and his family, and to Jaimin and Amandip Kotecha.

In Morocco, thanks to Richard and Sophie and Oliver Neat at the magnificent Casa Lalla in Marrakesh. In Lebanon, huge thanks to May and Nasser Nakib, and Talal Daouk for generously hosting us. A round of applause to Suha and to Kifah Arif for introductions to her family across the Middle East. Ronnie and Serj Hochar from Chateau Musar for their love of the flavors of life. In Jordan, Ali Najaf and family for a trip of wonders. In Turkey, Elizabeth Hewitt for being my eating companion, and Muhammet and Omer Solak for the incredible generosity of their family.

To the great cooks who have inspired me – Rose Gray and Ruth Rogers at the River Café, Rick Stein, Loyd Grossman, Peter Doyle from Est in Sydney, and David Thompson. To Tim Lee and Ashley Huntington for keeping the food debate wide open, Danielle and Rafael Fox Brinner, Bernie Plaisted (for being my best man in the kitchen), JJ Holland, Charlie Mash, Sarah Rowden, Clare Kelly, Birgit Erath and Celia Brooks Brown. To Chantal Rutherford Brown, the Cutting Edge School of Food and Wine, Books for Cooks, Susan Pieterse, Tertia Goodwin, all at Leiths, Liz Trigg, Toby Peters, Peter Durose, Helen Chislet. To Matt Maddocks, Wye Yap, Peter Harman, and everyone in Sydney. To Debbie Wallen, Annette Peters, and Helena Flemming at Marks & Spencer. To all the chefs and friends who make it so much fun. This is for you.

Picture Credits

The publisher would like to thank the following for their kind permission to reproduce their photographs:

(a-above; b-below; c-center; f-far; l-left; r-right; t top)

Alamy Images: Nick Baylis 40; Pat Behnke 140; Mike Booth 154; CuboImages srl 113bl, 113br; Danita Delimont 72; eStock Photo 62; Food Alan King 23br; Peter Forsberg 24; Doug Houghton 57; La Belle Aurore 31; Manor Photography 38; Adrian Muttitt 20, 36; PCL 23tl; Picture Contact 120; Robert Harding Picture Library Ltd 110; Alex Segre 35; Jochen Tack 76; Tribaleye Images / J Marshall 82; **Corbis:** zefa / Peter Adams 23tr; **Getty Images:** Gallo Images / Heinrich van den Berg 29; The Image Bank / Stuart Westmorland 23bl; Purestock 26; Robert Harding World Imagery / Amanda Hall 32; **PunchStock:** Brand X Pictures 169

All other travel images © Tom Kime

Jacket images: Front: Getty Images: The Image Bank / John Lund tr; Lonely Planet Images / Paul Beinssen ftr; National Geographic / Richard Nowitz ftl; Stone / Simon Watson tl

All other images © Dorling Kindersley

Thanks also to Magimix for equipment supplied for the photographic shoot.

For further information see: www.dkimages.com